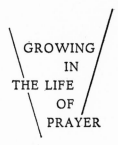

GROWING
IN
THE LIFE
OF
PRAYER

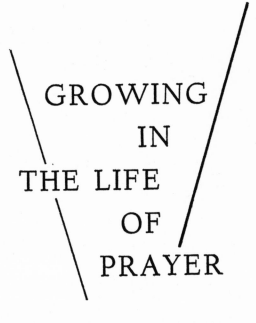

GROWING
IN
THE LIFE
OF
PRAYER

Harold Wiley Freer

Abingdon Press
NEW YORK • NASHVILLE

GROWING IN THE LIFE OF PRAYER

Copyright © 1962 by Abingdon Press

Library of Congress Catalog Card Number: 62-9384

Scripture quotations unless otherwise noted are
from the Revised Standard Version of the Bible
and are copyright 1946 and 1952 by the Di-
vision of Christian Education of the National
Council of the Churches of Christ in the U.S.A.

SET UP, PRINTED, AND BOUND BY THE
PARTHENON PRESS, AT NASHVILLE,
TENNESSEE, UNITED STATES OF AMERICA

Dedication

In I Sam. 10 is the story of the choosing of Saul to be the first king of Israel. Verse 26 says that after the choosing, Saul "went to his home at Gibeah, and with him went men of valor whose hearts God had touched."

This book is appreciatively dedicated to the host of men and women, ministers and lay folk, saints both living and dead, men and women of valor whose hearts God had touched, who through the years have walked with me and blessed me knowingly and unknowingly through their faith and love. Their untold number forbids the listing of their names.

PREFACE

Do you really seek to know the living God? Would you truly *work out* your own salvation with fear and trembling?

Here is a way of prayer by which you may become aware of the reality of his presence as you grow in communion with him and in understanding of yourself—for to know God is to know the self, and to know the self is to know God. It is a pipe that runs both ways, a realization of the eternal God that reveals oneself, and a discovery of the self that leads to awareness of Reality.

This approach is not for the casual person seeking excitement, the desultory one avoiding boredom, nor the curious one testing ways to "use" God. It is for the earnest seeker willing to discipline himself through careful practice of a series of exercises in mental prayer over a minimum of thirty-two weeks.

Far too many people think of prayer only as petition, getting something for themselves or for others. Petitionary prayer belongs to the kindergarten years of one's faith and practice. In its lowest form petition seeks material things for oneself or another. Even when it rises to requests for spiritual goods, the virtues, still it is essentially man's attempt to get from God something for himself or another. Hence, the self is at the center of such prayer, even though it does recognize God as the giver of all gifts.

These exercises in mental prayer are to take you beyond the kindergarten years into maturing ways of praying that will serve a twofold purpose: First, to help you keep God at the center of all your prayer;

7

and second, to help you understand your real self with its hindrances to self-knowledge and God-knowledge.

Each weekly lesson or chapter is divided into two parts, a meditation and an exercise. The meditations are written in the first person singular, prayers spoken directly to God. This is done to help you avoid saying "we" or "you all," and thus using the plural as alibi for yourself. "Thou art the man" is the emphasis of the meditations. They are highly personal; you are to listen to what God is saying to you, not to another. The meditations are not introspective, however. They look within only that you may look beyond yourself to God. You must move from self to him if you are to grow.

The exercises, week by week, progress through the six major kinds of maturing prayer—thanksgiving, confession, forgiveness, intercession, adoration, and commitment—with specific suggestions at the close of each for practice during the week ahead. Merely to read either meditation or exercise, and then to turn from them, would be valueless. They are to be read and studied and practiced.

These lessons may be used in either of two ways. An individual, in his own quiet time each day, may make them his own. He should read the meditation through slowly and thoughtfully, asking God's blessing upon that reading, then go back phrase by phrase, letting his mind follow the thoughts that God places there. Usually thirty minutes is long enough for each day's study. Then he should read the exercise for the week and immediately begin to put it into practice. The same meditation and exercise is then used daily for a week.

Sometimes one may wish to spend more than a week with an exercise, as he begins to understand himself better through his growing awareness of God. Each person will need to work this out according to his own *attrait*.

The second and probably the better way to use this material is within a small group gathered together as a weekly prayer class. It is rare for a person alone to persist in regular study. The pressure of his own busyness makes him forget one day—and that is the beginning of the end! When he shares regularly and punctually with others in a study class, however, their mutual encouragement will keep him on the way.

In most prayer classes that meet once a week, the hour together is divided into two periods—thirty minutes of silence, and thirty minutes of shared witness. During the silence the meditation for the week is used as the basic prayer. In the second period insights that have come from the meditation or experiences growing out of the practice of the previous week's exercise are shared.[1]

You will note that these meditations and exercises begin with the self. There is very little social concern at first, for the normal round of religious and churchly activities is an excellent way to escape both from oneself and from God. Not until after several weeks of encounter with the eternal God will you be led beyond yourself to others. First you must find the Way, and then, and then only, as the outcome of a God-centered life will your service be truly Christian.

These lessons are not a means to take you out of this world; rather, they are to put you into the very heart of it. Christianity from the days of its Founder has been a relationship—man with God, and man with his fellow man. So the intent of these lessons is to make relevant to this present day and this present world your awareness both of the eternal God and of your own true self.

—Harold Wiley Freer

---

[1] For a detailed description of technique in a prayer class, see pp. 83-86, in Harold W. Freer and Francis B. Hall, *Two or Three Together* (New York: Harper & Brothers, 1954), a manual for prayer groups used in more than 1,200 such classes.

CONTENTS

11

THE
FIRST WEEK

The Meditation

BLESSED ART THOU, O GOD. OUT OF THY MIND HAS COME FORTH THIS WORLD OF mine. Long before man put himself at the center of all life, thou didst create the heavens and the earth. Long before man began to lord it over thy creatures, thou didst hold them in the hollow of thy hand. From everlasting to everlasting thou art God.

Great and majestic is thy way. Through the multitude of the years thou hast caused the mountains to stand forth in all their grandeur. Thou hast gathered together the waters into the hollows of the earth, tiny lakes and mighty seas. Thou hast spangled the heavens with distant stars.

Upon the face of this thy earth, thou hast brought forth life. With spore and spawn thou hast sprinkled the valleys and the plains, dark forests and verdant prairies speaking of thy glory. How hast thou made them? And why? Far beyond my comprehension is thy creativity. Far beyond my finite mind is thy infinite mind.

Yet thou dost reveal thyself to me, thy creature. Deep within my spirit, thy spirit speaks to me. Deep within my longings, my desires, my hopes, thou dost call me to thyself. I look unto thee, and thou art found. I cry unto thee, and thou dost respond.

I would know thee, I would love thee, I would worship thee. Thou art my Father, and I am thy child. Give me of thyself that I may give

15

myself to thee. Pour into the tiny drop of myself the vast ocean of thyself.

What We Mean by Mental Prayer

In this series of laboratory exercises in the practice of mental prayer we will learn to pray inwardly. We are not interested in words as such. In time we will leave words behind us. We will come to know firsthand Paul's prayer without ceasing, which is mental prayer.

Mental prayer is the heart speaking to God. Only as we truly desire do we truly pray. The desiring heart, the longing heart, finds God.

> As a deer longs for the water-courses,
> So my whole being longs for thee, O God.
> My whole being thirsts for God, for the living God.[1]
> (Ps. 42:1-2a, Smith-Goodspeed)

"Prayer," said Thomas Aquinas, "is the interpreter of a desire." With desire Jesus prayed, "Abba, Father, all things are possible to thee; remove this cup from me." But with even greater desire he went on to pray, "Yet not what I will, but what thou wilt." (Mark 14:36.)

This is the prayer of commitment, the prayer of self-abandonment. The whole self in all its fullness and in all its emptiness makes its complete self-offering to him. We would love him with all our hearts and souls and minds and strength. To be one with God—this is our whole prayer.

To be one with him, however, we must know him. We must know him as the God of love whose true self is revealed in Jesus Christ. We must know him as the God of all creation, the Creator, of whose creatures man is but one among many. We must know him as the living God, the Eternal Spirit before whom we become lost in adoration. We

---

[1] Copyright 1939 by the University of Chicago.

must know him as the intimate Friend with whom we may have affectionate converse.

Through mental prayer we grow in knowledge of this One as he gives of himself through grace. The acts of thanksgiving, of adoration, of faith and hope and love, which we offer to him draw us closer to him. We love him as we know him better, and we know him better as we love him more. As Saint Bonaventure has written: "In mental prayer the mind alone unfolds its desires before God, pouring forth to Him the affections of the heart, interiorly clinging to Him by love and reverently adoring Him." "Words, because of their inadequacy," he goes on to say, "are not used, for the more completely the soul empties itself into God the deeper go the affections and the less ability one has of expressing them." So he comes to his conclusion: "Pure mental prayer is made when the lips move not, but the heart speaks to God." [2]

For most of us words will be necessary in the beginning of our prayer, words thought if not spoken. The time will come, though, when the attitude of prayer—that of thanksgiving, of forgiveness, of intercession, of adoration—will be part of our very being, the soul emptied into God. Until then, we will need words, through deliberate choice and conscious effort, to express our deepening desire.

As a foundation for all mental prayer, we begin our laboratory exercises with prayer for others. Make your own prayer list. If you are in a prayer class the members of that class will head your list. Add to this the members of your immediate family, friends for whom you may have a special concern, others whom God will send to you as you learn to offer them in intercession to him. In your quiet time each day pray by name for each one, offering them to God in love. See each person in your mind's eye as though he is surrounded by the light of God's love. Hold him in your attention until all other objects or thoughts disappear and he alone is in that light. Then pass on to the next person on your list.

[2] Bede Frost, *The Art of Mental Prayer* (New York: Harper & Brothers), p. 73.

When you have completed your list of persons, offer in love the minister and congregation of your church as they come together in corporate worship on the Sunday next. See them as a worshiping people, quietly and reverently waiting before God. Expect him to speak through the acts of worship. Then attend the service on Sunday with expectation.

Remember to practice these two exercises of intercession in your quiet time each day without fail. Then two things will happen. First, you will be taken out of yourself. You will begin to think of others in Christian love. You will begin laying the groundwork for the prayer that is love and the love that is prayer. This is the first step in loving your neighbor as yourself.

Second, you become part of a living fellowship, the Body of Christ that is the Church. You are not alone in your search to be one with God, nor do you follow an unknown way. In company with others you travel a well-marked path, whose guideposts are the great hymns and prayers and scriptures and liturgies through which folk in humble chapels and in towering cathedrals have found God.

THE
SECOND WEEK

The Meditation

I COME UNTO THEE, O GOD, AS A SEARCHER FOR A WAY OF LIFE THAT WILL mean fulfillment for me. With open mind and willing heart I would learn of thee as I share this fellowship. Forgive me if at first I seem quite selfish, seeking my own gain. I need understanding of myself, my hopes, my desires, my longings. Help me to see where self does come first, that I may use that self, not to glorify nor enhance it, but to bring it under the control of thy greater Self.

Forbid, O God, that anything I learn here should set me apart from others. Humble me ere pride in this group should make me snobbish or "certain of my arrival." Teach me how to take into my daily living the truths thou dost give me, that in home, in community, in church, at work and at play, with my doubt and with my faith, I may reveal the best that thou dost grant unto me. I would truly learn of thee that I may be a better child of thy spirit, a better neighbor in love—neighbor to those in my home, those next door to me, those in far places.

Help me to find answers that will open the fullness of thy spirit to me.

What is it I want most for myself?

How can the little I have be used in a world of change?

What sources of strength have I found in thee that I can share with others in this fellowship? With members of my family at home? With my friends?

What is my deepest need?

Grant, O God, that with keen mind and with warm heart, with the best of my thinking, and the fullness of my affection, I may be drawn to thee and to these others in this fellowship. I turn unto thee as a pitcher brought to a fountain. Fill me with thy living water.

Awareness of God Through Prayer

We are not interested primarily in knowing *about* God. Books of philosophy and theology will answer some of our questions about him. We are interested in *knowing* him. To know God is to commune with him. Prayer is one way to commune with him, for prayer *is* communion.

Through art, through music, and through nature, as well as through prayer, folk have learned to commune with God. For most of us prayer is the one supreme avenue to God, by which we may become aware of his presence. Through prayer we talk with him, love him, even serve him.

We may begin largely with monologue, doing all the talking ourselves. Often we need to pour out our thoughts to him, just as at times we overwhelm a friend with the rush of words through which we find emotional release. A good conversationalist does not monopolize the talk, however; he learns to listen too.

More and more as we practice the art of mental prayer we will learn to listen, to hear God speaking to us in the inner depth of our being. As we grow in the life of prayer, we will gradually approach monologue again, but this time it will be God who will speak, we who listen. In time, for some of us, our communion will be like the farmer who came to the church at Ars to pray. Once a neighbor asked him what he was doing so long in church. The old Père Chaffangeon replied: "I am looking at God, and God is looking at me."

This awareness of God begins with conscious effort on our part. Once I was absorbed with writing at my desk when suddenly I felt a tugging at my sleeve. "Daddy, I'm here," declared my small daughter when I looked around. How long she had been there, I don't know, but I had to make a conscious effort to look up from my work to be aware of her. In similar fashion we need to look up from our busyness to become aware of the drawing of God's spirit. As we grow in awareness conscious effort will no longer be so important. In the deep consciousness we will be aware of him. But until that time comes we will need to work at it persistently.

Here is the true meaning of the parables of Jesus about the neighbor at midnight of Luke 11:5-8 and the importunate widow of Luke 18:1-8. We do not change God by our persistent prayer—as though he needs to be cajoled into serving us! Rather, we need to work at our praying until it changes us, for only as we truly desire do we truly pray, as we have already learned. We can grow just as much as we wish if we will work at it. Jesus believed this when he prayed, "I do not pray for these only, but also for those who are to believe in me through their word, that they may all be one; even as thou, Father, art in me, and I in thee, that they also may be in us." (John 17:20-21.) There is our prayer: To be one with him.

To achieve through his grace this prayer we will practice certain forms of prayer through these weeks ahead. First is the prayer of thanksgiving, an awareness of God's bounty and love. Second is the prayer of confession, an awareness of the self in its inadequacy and sin. Third is the prayer of forgiveness, an awareness of God's pardon. In each of these love from God is revealed. In his love he has given to us of his bounty; he has revealed to us our true selves; he has offered to us his pardon. In response to love *from* him we make our prayer.

That is not sufficient, however. We also offer love *to* him through three other forms of prayer. First is the prayer of intercession, an awareness of the needs of others offered to God. Second is the prayer of adoration, an awareness of the glory of God. Third is the prayer of commitment, an awareness of the need for fulfillment. In each of these our love to God is revealed. In thankfulness to him for the gift of his love to us we offer our friends to him in intercession, we adore him, we give ourselves to him in self-abandonment.

Before we begin the practice of these exercises in prayer, however, let us ask ourselves how we have learned up to this point to be aware of God's presence.

For many of us nature is a revelation of God. Recall times of awareness, times when you knew something of the awe and the majesty of the Creator as seen in the world of nature. Were these times always related to the spectacular—a visit to Niagara, to the Grand Canyon, or to the ocean? Or have you seen his hand in simple awareness of the wonder of growing grass and nesting birds and blooming flowers?

At what times and in what places did the doors of music open for you into his presence? In great symphonies and colorful operas and stirring marches we have been deeply moved. But have not our hearts been strangely warmed too by a haunting spiritual or a mother's lullaby or a youth's frenetic syncopation through jazz?

What were the poems that spoke of God? How has some painting surprised you with the joy of his presence? Before what sculpture have you stood in humble meditation as you became one with the spirit of the sculptor? In simple chapels and ornate sanctuaries has God touched your heart?

In what other ways have you been aware of the presence of the living God?

THE
THIRD WEEK

The Meditation

WHEN THY HAND FALLS UPON ME, O GOD, LIGHT THOUGH ITS TOUCH MAY be, I know.

Sometimes it comes in judgment. A sense of guilt like a creeping blush slips over my consciousness, and I am ill at ease. I cannot look another in the eye, and I try to hide from thee. In shocking awareness I see myself as I truly am, a sinner who has done wrong in thy sight—disobedient, disloyal, unloving. I have been thinking only of myself, of my desires. I am ashamed, ashamed before thee.

Sometimes thy hand is a compelling one, pushing me until I say: "I will arise and go." In fear of what others may say, in fear of my own inability, I hold back from doing what I know I should do. In lethargy of spirit I put off doing today what I imagine will be easier, less troublesome, more "inspired" to do in another day. In loneliness of heart I hesitate to speak forth the truth thou hast revealed to me, lest I stand erect in the land of the hunchbacks. But thy touch is a burning within me, a fire that I cannot quench. Moved by the urgency of thy spirit within, I rise up.

Sometimes the wonder of life, its awe, its mystery, overflows me. Like Moses of old I draw the mantle of myself around me, unable to look into thy face. But thou hast passed by—in the comradeship of a friend, in the love of a man for a woman, in the hush of a still evening after storm, in the freedom of an unfettered child, in the motionless flight of a nectar-seeking hummingbird, in the birth of a babe, in the death of a friend. Down upon the knees of my spirit I drop in awesome dread.

Sometimes thy joy and peace enfold me, and I sing forth thy praise. Not for the blessings that I have received at thy hand, nor for those blessings which lie ahead, do I lift my heart in adoration; but for thyself alone, the living God, I bless thy holy name.

Yea, when thy hand falls upon me, O God, light though its touch may be, I know!

Renewing Our Wonder

His lips twisted with scorn. "I know all about that!" he said. His teacher looked at the ten-year-old lad with concern.

"You know all about everything!" the teacher replied. "Doesn't anything interest you?" she asked. She had tried to win the boy's attention, but she had failed.

On the playground he wouldn't join the other boys in their make-believe games. They were silly. In the craft class he didn't want to work with leather or wood or beads. "Only girls do that," he pointed out.

His cub master and his den mother talked together about him. No matter what they tried, no matter how excited the other boys became, Horace sniffed in disdain. "I know all about that!" was his continual reply.

When Horace moved from that community his teachers and his scout leaders sighed with puzzled relief, puzzled because they could not understand where they had failed. No other ten-year-old in their experience was so blasé, so lacking in wonder. Nothing fazed Horace. He was as cold as the proverbial chunk of ice. He had seen everything, done everything.

Unfortunately, Horace began to lose his sense of wonder earlier than most of us. We too have seen most everything, done most everything. "What's new?" is more than a colloquial question asked at the corner bus stop. It reveals the hunger of our jaded spirits for something unusual, bizarre, extraordinary. Like Samuel Goldwyn of Hollywood fame, who hoped to create a colossal motion picture by beginning with an earthquake, then moving to a climax, we would build startling event upon more startling event, until we run out of startles. Then we fall back into boredom, waiting for some new fad or fashion or fancy to stimulate our wonderless day.

How does it happen that we have lost our sense of wonder? Is it because we have so many things these days? Small boys a generation ago played their version of football with a sack full of dirty rags, but boys today demand professional footballs, helmets, sweaters—even a playing field. The former went out and made their equipment and then enjoyed their game. The latter expect it all to be handed to them, as part of their "due." Are we adults surfeited by the multiplicity of things, so that we have lost our wonder?

Remember the summer picnics by the "ole swimmin' hole"? Remember how the kinsfolk would come on Sunday afternoon, everyone sharing in turning the heavy handle of the ice cream freezer? Remember the visiting missionary whose stories of Africa held us enthralled as a whole new world was opened up to us in Sunday school once a year or so? Remember the piano player whose nimble fingers accompanied the old silent movies, causing us to weep or to beat our feet in excitement? Few of us do remember those things any more. Weren't those the good old days?

No! They were not. Wonder was there, as all of us who had "exciting" parents or zestful teachers know. But they were no better days than today, if with shining eyes we look out upon our world.

Day after day Deirdre watched with increasing wonder until late into the fall, announcing with delight, "The hummingbirds are still here!" It was a month past their usual departure time for their winter homes in Central America. Then on October sixteenth she reported no hummingbirds so far that day. The next day she still could not find any. She thought about it for a while, then asked with puzzlement, "Daddy, how do they know when to leave? And how do they know their way to Central America?" Who can answer that question?

When Job thought he knew all the answers, God asked him a few questions: "Where were you when the foundations of the earth were laid? Who shut in the sea with doors? Where is the way to the dwelling of light?" (See Job 38–39.)

There is still mystery in life. Awe and wonder are basic to our appreciative understanding of the way of the Creator. Surely enough, the birds migrate. How do they know when and where to go? Surely enough, boy meets girl. Who can describe what one "sees" in the other? The youth with limitless energy is soon outmaneuvered by the elder with his controlled power. Why? The good man suffers and the careless man prospers. Why?

Take time to sit down with folk who know wonder. Go first where little children are at play. Watch a child laugh with glee when first he ties his shoe strings. Open your eyes with wonder as his open with the sight of a butterfly coming from its chrysalis. Kneel with him as he studies the ants in his play yard. Try to be a pokerface when a motley crew of lively boys and girls rise to sing like angels as the children's choir shares a service of worship.

Then seek out a man or a woman who loves the things of nature. Listen to him speak of the birds, of the stars, of the flowers and the trees. Catch a glimpse of his enthusiasm—his en-theos, his in-God—as he describes the wonder of nature. Listen to a man whose delight is in words—the clothing of poetry, of drama, of simple folk tales whose telling leaves the mouth partly open in rapt attention.

Go alone into the heart of a forest, climb a small hill on a clear night bright with stars, or walk in the midst of a busy city crowd and feel the wonder of life in all its fullness.

Then jot down moments of wonder you recall from the past and match each of them with one from the present. Let these be your sacrifices of joy as you offer yourself to God with praise and thanksgiving at the close of your day.

THE
FOURTH WEEK

The Meditation

I BELIEVE; FORGIVE THOU MY UNBELIEF. I BELIEVE THAT IN THY HANDS is my life. I believe that in thy love is the meaning of my life. I believe that in thy will is the purpose of my life. But I am not sure, O God, that I am ready to place myself wholly and completely in thy care.

I need thy help, and I want thy help; yet in the depths of my being I wonder if I really would accept thy help. If I am to give myself in full commitment to thee I must change my ways of living, of thinking, of loving. Am I willing to change, to be wholly thine, to forget myself and my own desires?

I would stand upon my own, thinking for myself, acting for myself. I do not wish to be dependent upon another—not even upon thee. Yet I cannot stand on my own, for I am limited by my own finiteness. Am I willing to go as far as I can go with my own strength, my own wisdom, my own ability; then to give myself wholly into thy hands, to accept from thee thy strength, thy wisdom, thy love?

Thou knowest that time and again I need direction. The way is dark or the path is uncertain. Yet I would rather stumble along in my pride than admit, even to thee, that I do not know all the answers, that I am not sure of all the turns. Am I willing to walk to the edge of my knowledge, then trust in thy providence as I move into the unknown?

In truth I would take thy power into myself that I may be strong.

Though I know that I can of myself do little—I can hardly say "I can do nothing"—yet at the same time I believe I can do all things through thee. But I doubt if I want to do all things through thee! Still do I hold to myself, to my own strength, to my own pride.

O God, Thou knowest my doubt and fear. I am trying to be honest with thee and with myself. Grant to me insight to see that my true freedom will come when I give to thee my whole self. Grant me courage to act upon that insight. O God, thou knowest my little faith; enlarge it in thy mercy.

Take Nothing for Granted

(THANKSGIVING—1)

Prayers of thanksgiving are an awareness of God's bounty and love. They are the spontaneous cries of an appreciative heart, grateful for God's limitless gifts.

> Bless the Lord, O my soul;
>   and all that is within me, bless his holy name!
> Bless the Lord, O my soul;
>   and forget not all his benefits.

For most of us his gifts are taken for granted. We expect them to be given to us and speak up only when we do not receive them. How seldom we thank him for the many beautiful days, though we usually complain about the infrequent stormy ones! If we were to treat our husbands or wives in the same casual way that we treat God, how long would our marriages last? We dare not take others for granted as we do the Creator of all life, lest we lose our friends and alienate people. We become casual, blasé, thoughtless in our acceptance of God's gifts.

No child does this. Everything is new, wonderful, to a small child. His laughter surrounds his day with delight as each event surprises him. Mr. Ilo Orleans, in his volume of childhood poetry *This Wonderful Day,* has captured much of this delight in his poem "All My Senses":

> I stand beside the doorway,
>   And what do you think *I hear?*
> The chirp-chirp-chirp of grasshoppers
>   Which sound so very near!
>
> I walk around the garden,
>   And what do you think *I smell?*
> Magnolia, mint, and lilac,
>   And rose and coral-bell!
>
> I sit at the breakfast table,
>   And what do you think *I taste?*
> My cereal, and buttered toast—
>   Good food I must not waste!
>
> I *touch* the stones by the lily-pond,
>   And what do you think *I feel?*
> The soft green moss—as silky smooth
>   As the fur of a baby seal!
>
> I look outside the window,
>   And what do you think *I see?*
> A robin, hop-hop-hopping
>   Beneath the maple tree!
>
> I'm happy I have ears and nose
>   And tongue and hands and eyes!
> With *all my senses* I enjoy
>   The world that round me lies.[1]

[1] New York: Union of American Hebrew Congregations, 1958, pp. 10-11. Used by permission.

Just as some children on Thanksgiving Day make a list of things for which to be thankful, so we adults need to list evidences of God's love. Marie wished that she might have an awareness of God's presence similar to that of some in her prayer class. As we sat together facing her kitchen window I called her attention to the potted geraniums on the sill, the bright red blossoms with the dark green leaves. In the background was the intense blue of the autumn sky, with white clouds passing by. All was framed by dainty curtains of soft yellow. "Thank God for the colorful window in your 'workroom,'" I suggested. "I hadn't thought of that," she replied. "Then when the four children come rushing in from the school bus at four and hurry to the refrigerator, thank him again for their appetites." "They are hungry when they get home," she said. "About six your husband will be coming in. He has worked hard so that you and your family might have this first home of your own. Thank God for Pat and his devotion to all of you." "I've never done that," she said quietly.

"Do this every day," I told her. "Then add others for whom you can thank God. And see how many things you can thank him for."

Six weeks later she visited with relatives in New England. "Many times I have been there," she reported, "when the color of the mountains was gorgeous, but suddenly on this trip I felt a deep sense of the presence of God which I never had before." Some eighteen months later she told a group of friends about this same experience, adding that from that visit until the present time she knew something of the wonder of God's presence in the world about her. With deliberate prayers of thanksgiving persistently offered she had come to this awareness.

Like Marie we need consciously to list things for which to be thankful, and then to offer our thanksgiving. Like her we may list the ordinary objects around our homes, the clouds, the sky, the stars, the grass, the flowers, the trees, the birds. A little girl paid her father a high compliment by asking when she came home from school,

"Daddy, what did you find that was new today?" Then he told her of a blue-tailed lizard, of a woodpecker putting acorns in a metal clothesline pole, of a walking stick that climbed the screen door. For each of these, and more, both of them were thankful.

Consider the thumb. Reach it across to the other fingers. Only man and the monkeys can do that. Our civilization rests largely upon man's ability to reach across with his thumb, making it possible for him to grasp the tools to build, to farm, to cook. For the humble thumb, God's gift to us, few of us ever have been thankful.

This week begin to list day by day objects of nature for which you are grateful. Over and over again lift quick little prayers of thanksgiving for the beauty of a fair day, the dark colorings of a stormy one, the heat of the sun, the coolness of a gentle breeze, the wonder of a tree. Consciously offer prayers of thanksgiving in pauses throughout the day, searching for items in the wonder and glory of nature for which to bless God. The more one practices thanksgiving the more one turns from self-pity, from boredom, from depression. Fill each day of the week with quick thrusts of simple thanks to God as he is revealed in nature.

THE
FIFTH WEEK

The Meditation

O THOU NAMELESS ONE, WHOM I CANNOT CONTAIN IN A SINGLE WORD,
forgive the inadequacy of my speech. Thou art more than all my thinking, greater than all my imagining. Thou art beyond the farthest
reaches of my mind, the deepest longings of my heart. Yet I would
know thee, the Unknowable One.

Creator of all life thou art, from the tiniest of amoebas to the largest
of mammals, from the first protoplasmic cells with directive purpose
to the complex human beings who seek to be one with thee. Out of
thy mind have come forth the worlds known and unknown; and
time and space, creatures of man's need, are as nothing to thee. What
is man, that thou art mindful of him? Or the son of man, that thou
visiteth him?

God thou art, the living God. God of Abraham, Isaac, and Jacob,
God of the prophets, God of the psalmists, thou art my God. God of my
grandparents, God of my children, my God—thou art the living God.
In thee I live and move and have my being.

Father of my Lord Jesus Christ and my Father! With daring of
spirit I so name thee, for I am thy child, created in thy image. I cannot
be content only to bow before thee in awe and wonder, awesome
though thou art. In trembling of hope I seek beyond thy majesty and
grandeur one whom I may love, one who will love me.

I believe thou art love. I believe thou dost care for me as a father cares for his children. I believe thou dost give thyself to me through thy Son, Jesus Christ. I believe thou dost dwell in the innermost parts of my being. I believe I may know thee in spirit and in truth.

Yea, thou art the Nameless One, whom I have tired to hold for a moment in a word of my choosing. Creative Energy, *Elan Vital,* Eternal Spirit, the Holy One of Israel, God Almighty, Father—all describe but a small portion of thee. Wonder of wonders, thou hast revealed thyself to me, and I *do* know thee. Blessed be thy name.

Speak to Him thou for He hears, and Spirit with Spirit can meet— Closer is He than breathing, and nearer than hands and feet.

"These Touched My Life!"

(THANKSGIVING—2)

One of the most suggestive of verses is I Sam. 10:26, concluding the choosing of Saul to be the first king of Israel. Samuel presented Saul to the people, giving them instructions concerning the rights and duties of a king, after which he sent them all to their various homes. Then the story says "Saul also went to his home at Gibeah, and with him went men of valor whose hearts God had touched."

When I was a growing lad I heard a neighbor ask my mother: "Have you decided what you want your four sons to be?" "No," my mother replied. "I am not going to choose for them. My one hope is that each one becomes a man." Whether or not I have become a man is for others to say, but this I know: Whatever manhood is mine is largely due to the love and care of my father and mother. They were "men of valor whose hearts God had touched."

All through my ministry as a pastor and teacher I have been surrounded by patient, devoted, loyal laymen and lay women. Through those years God has blessed that simple ministry through the "men of valor" who have shared with me the life and work of our churches.

Whatever creative work has been done through those years rests largely upon the "men of valor" who went with me, as together our hearts were touched by God.

Mrs. John Pickard was the wife of a railroad section laborer. In her home was a four-shelf bookcase in which she kept books from a Carnegie library in a nearby city. To her home came a teen-ager hungry for books, and as soon as he read through the lot, she went off to the city to get a new selection for him. For two years, as long as his parents lived in that rural area, she stuffed him with good books. Years later he wrote her a letter of appreciation for the strong diet with which she had fed his hungry spirit. He never will forget her. It is as George Bernard Shaw wrote at the death of William Morris: "You can lose a man like that by your own death, but not by his."

William Shegog was principal of a small high school in a mining community. To a shy junior Mr. Shegog came during study hall and talked about literature and politics and world affairs as though the lad were a mature traveler from distant parts with ideas of his own to share with simple provincials. Confidence and assurance became his as the selfless teacher shared with him.

A freshman returning to his room one Saturday afternoon from a hike in the marshes nearby met Professor Rollin H. Walker. "Your boots say you have been tramping in the marshes," the professor said.

"Yes," the college student replied, "and I found a red-winged blackbird's nest." "I took a picture of it," he reported with pleasure.

"For your zoology course?" the professor wanted to know.

"No, I just took it for myself."

"You must be a member of the bird-study course."

"No, I just went out on my own."

"You didn't go out to fulfill a requirement?"

"No, I just went out on my own."

"Then it was just between you and God this day," Dr. Walker said. Just what did he mean? Many times since then that boy has wondered about that conversation. Out of it has grown an interest in birds and trees and the world of nature, not to "fulfill a requirement," but to enjoy a small part of the wonder of "my Father's world."

Write down this week the names of parents, of brothers and sisters, of other kinsfolk, putting beside their names some of the gifts that they have given you as they walked along with you in your growing days. Recall a schoolteacher, a neighbor, a classmate, whose simple gifts to you, often unbeknown to them, you will never forget. Thank God for each of these persons, men and women of valor "whose hearts God has touched," remembering each of them individually. Let your meditation each day be filled with new faces as you thank God for these specific ones whose lives have touched yours.

Perhaps you will want to visit one of these persons, telling him briefly something of the way in times past God through him has blessed you. You will be surprised how much such a visit will mean to an older person whose friends are becoming fewer and fewer in number each year.

You may wish to write a thank-you note to someone. Its surprise will brighten his day and encourage his work. How seldom do we know when something we have said and done touches another. The grace of God hides these from us, lest we boast in our good works, but he permits us to be his mail men, carrying letters from him.

Do not forget your present companions, members of your own household, business associates, searchers with you in your study groups, others who walk along with you in these days. Offer a prayer of thanksgiving for these by name, being quite specific as you enumerate those qualities in them for which you are thankful.

With these prayers of thanksgiving filling your days this week, you will come to know something of what Walt Whitman meant when he wrote:

Why should I wish to see God better than this day?

I see something of God each hour of the twenty-four, and each moment then,
In the faces of men and women I see God, and in my own face in the glass;
I find letters from God dropt in the street, and every one is sign'd by God's
    name,
And I leave them where they are, for I know that wheresoe'er I go,
Others will punctually come for ever and ever.

THE
SIXTH WEEK

The Meditation

THANKS BE UNTO THEE, O GOD, FOR THE FELLOWSHIP OF THOSE WHO search for thee. Without their encouragement, without their discipline, without their seeking, I would find it almost insuperable to continue on my way. Nothing brings such loneliness to me as my inability to make others understand the ferment of my spirit as it longs for thee. But thou hast shown me others whose spirits too would know thee, and in them do I find my delight.

Time and again I have picked up a book and deep has spoken to deep, and I have known thee with sharper awareness because of the testimony of an author who now becomes a companion of the spirit. A man or a woman who knows thee has touched my growing edge, and through his writings thou dost enlarge my heart and mind.

How often have I gone half-heartedly to a religious gathering, hardly daring to believe that thou wouldst be there, only to be surprised by thy words in the voice of one unknown, who from that time becomes a fellow seeker of thy truth. How grateful I am to thee, O God, for these seemingly casual meetings that reveal once again thy strange providence. In out-of-the-way places and at the oddest times thou leadest me to others who hunger and thirst for thee, and together we feast upon thy love.

Alone I might continue my search. Alone I might come to understand myself as I really am. Alone I might know thee in oneness of spirit.

But I have not been alone. Thou hast helped to find others eager to know thee, ready to learn of thee, willing to share their findings. How great is the blessing that has been mine because of their friendship! Through them I have been made bold to press on, to wrestle with myself and with thee.

Blessed art thou, O God, for the cloud of thy witnesses with which thou hast surrounded me. Continue thy love to me in confronting me by thy spirit in the lives of others, for in the blessed fellowship of thy saints do I find my strength and my joy.

Fruits of the Spirit

(THANKSGIVING—3)

"But the fruit of the Spirit is love, joy, peace, patience, kindness, goodness, faithfulness, gentleness, self-control." (Gal. 5:22.)

For two weeks now we have been experimenting with prayers of thanksgiving. We have been filling our days with gratitude and appreciation for the gifts of God to us through nature and through people. We have looked about us with fresh understanding, seeing what we had not seen before. Already we are learning to lift up quick glances of thanksgiving throughout the day to the One whose gifts have been spread out before us in such abundance.

Why do most people offer their thanksgiving almost entirely for material, tangible gifts alone? To the seeing eye God's gifts of the spiritual, the intangible, are in even greater abundance.

Not only are the fruits of the spirit in greater abundance, in truth they are also far more important. Consider the gourmet able financially to eat regularly in expensive restaurants or to engage high-salaried cooks to prepare special delicacies. Does his joy come from eating these foods alone? Or is it in having a companion with whom to share his delight? For most folk it is far better to have simple food and companionship than the finest of exotic dishes and loneliness.

39

Companionship is much more than the physical presence of another person. True love is not the delight of a man in the appearance of his wife, in her attractive clothing, in her shapeliness, nor in her usefulness to him in the kitchen, the living room, and the bedroom. True love is the awareness of a person, not for what he does but what he is. True love begins when the important question "Do you love me?" is no longer necessary. Verbal assurance gives way to certainty. One *knows*.

So it is with the gift of God's love. "If he loves me, then he should see that I have all that I need, even all I desire." That is the statement of one who loves not God, but his physical gifts. Some of us know his love apart from his gifts. Just that God *is*—this is the most profound of all knowledge. The certainty of his faithfulness, the assurance of his providence—which has nothing to do with the elimination of sickness, of hunger, of unemployment, or of any other limitations of physical care alone—the wonder of his ways, the intimacy of his revelation; these are but the beginning of his love far beyond physical gifts.

The very choice to love—to love our families, to love our friends, to love life, to love the world about us—is a gift of the Spirit. In our own feeble attempts we often come to a sorry end, as we try to bend love to our own pursuits. Robert Raynolds said:

Made as we are, we falter and fail, and do not continually do the work of love. But the work of love never passes; its mold is forever. The touch of God between I and Thou, which is love, never passes. We say people change, people part, love comes to an end. But we would be nothing if we had never done the work of love. If we had never once fulfilled a moment of life by the total offering and acceptance of life in God's presence, we would be nothing. Having loved never passes. We, even as we are, bear the eternal touch of having loved and having been loved.

We would more nearly fulfill all our lives if we would more often choose to love and do the work of love.

And to choose to love is to ask God how to love; He alone, and He always, reveals it.[1]

Each one of us has known moments of deep inner peace in the midst of the turmoil, the confusion, the noise, of our daily lives. Their joy has surrounded that turmoil and confusion and has quieted the noise. The problems were no fewer in number and no less difficult, but they could be faced out of tranquillity and boldness. We did not have additional physical resources; we did lay hold of the Source of all power.

What more can be said about joy and peace and patience and gentleness and others of the fruits of the Spirit? Make a list of these spiritual gifts, recalling times of kindness to you, especially by strangers or casual acquaintances; recalling acts of goodness, not because you were someone deserving such acts, but because the person himself was good.

Offer prayers of thanksgiving for his gift to you of patience, realizing that within yourself only impatience has its dwelling. Thank him that you have learned, even though infrequently, to control yourself, your appetites, your desires, even your longings, as you place them all in his hands.

Forgetting the many material gifts that are yours and laying behind you the physical evidence of God's love for you, lift your prayers of thanksgiving to him for himself, for who and what he is. This will be the beginning of true knowledge both of him and of yourself.

[1] *The Choice to Love* (New York: Harper & Brothers, 1959), pp. 92-93. Used by permission.

THE
SEVENTH WEEK

The Meditation

HOW HAS GOD BLESSED ME THIS WEEK?

I have had work to do, not being forced to sit idly. I have enjoyed fellowship within my family, both a physical nearness and a spiritual awareness of even deeper relationships. I have friends whose encouragement and understanding make light my day. I have routine to follow, so that a complete newness each day does not overwhelm me.

I have the world in its beauty to see, to hear, to touch, to taste, to smell. How colorful is each day, how pungent the wind rising from the earth. Birds in their flight, animals in their play, even the spider in its silk-spun trap, speak of thee. Full to overflowing is my cup, as I sense thy glory in the world about me.

In my quiet and in my busyness thou hast spoken to me. In my solitude and in my companionship thou hast been with me. Yet what have I done that I should deserve this? Freely thou givest me of thy love and thy strength without merit on my part. Accept thou my love and devotion. Increase my faith in thy strength. Help me to share in gratitude thy outpouring of love.

> Bless the Lord, O my soul;
> and all that is within me, bless his holy name.

On the Spiritual Frontier

(LOVE IN ACTION—1)

Miss Olga Deterding, daughter of a London multimillionaire, bored with the social rounds of England and the continent, went on safari to central Africa. Because of travel difficulties the safari party broke up—but she decided to go on alone. Quite by "accident" she came to Lambaréné, and visited the famous hospital there. She liked what she saw. Noting the selflessness of the staff and captured by the personality of Albert Schweitzer, she sought permission to stay. She was given a job in the scullery, where her hands learned to prepare food for the patients and the staff.

When the London newspapers found out where she was they reported her action, so that reporters from over the world sought her story. Consistently she refused to give out any word, and through the co-operation of Dr. Schweitzer no interviews were permitted at Lambaréné itself to sensation-hungry writers. Miss Deterding gave herself humbly and freely to service at Lambaréné in gratitude for the selflessness and love she found there. She was beginning to find purpose for her own life.

Few of us are able to leave our present homes and work for such "glamorous" service. If you are one of those who can leave, however, in gratitude to God and in service to man, are you willing to give yourself for a term as a teacher, an agriculturist, a business manager, a doctor, a librarian, to serve in a mission station at home or abroad? Through your own denominational board you may discover the opportunities for one with your qualifications. Study to learn if you are willing to accept new foods, strange customs, difficult situations, lonely isolation in the name of and for the glory of God and his love.

It is not necessary at all to go to a foreign land, however. Home-mission schools and colleges, inner-city parishes, rural experimental farms, retreat and conference centers, urban coffee houses among the unchurched, are but a few of the places where dedicated people, mature enough to go beyond status-seeking needs, may give themselves on new frontiers of the spirit in bringing Christian faith relevantly to American culture. Salaries are small; recognition is almost nil; the work is hard; misunderstandings are certain among former "friends"; but the rewards are "out of this world."

Most of us, however, are not called in any way to such action. We have responsibilities that hold us lovingly to our present homes and tasks, but we long to show through those homes and in those tasks our gratitude for the love of God to us. How can we do this?

Mrs. F was elected president of her church woman's society. Early in the fall she refused the invitation of her minister to enroll in a new prayer class. She expected to be too busy through the fall and winter. During the Christmas holidays, however, she asked to be a member of a new class being started. "Don't you want to know why?" she asked her minister. He gladly said he wanted to know why the change of mind.

"In September," she said, "I asked quite a few women to serve with me on committees of the woman's society, and they refused with various excuses. Last month in desperation I went again to some of them in my need for help, and that time several said they would help. Then I found out that every one who said she would help in December was a member of the prayer class. If a little more than two months of such classes will change women like that, I want to be in a class too!"

Serving on woman's society or men's club committees may not be your idea of serving God. Be careful, though, that you do not condescend to those who are willing so to serve. Find for yourself those places of service that will fit your temperament and your personality. You may run for election to the school board or the town council. You may accept scout leadership for boys or girls. You may teach Sunday afternoons in a mission church. You may seek to gather some cronies together for a monthly discussion group or a weekly prayer class—folk who have never thought that being Christian meant anything more than casual attendance at occasional church services or offhand contributions to an annual budget.

Better yet, in your home, your office, your store, your farm, or your classroom you may begin to practice a life of thanksgiving, of appreciation.

Ask yourself, What can I do with what I have, right here where I am, to serve him? Then begin first with the Jews, then the Gentiles—first with those in your own household, your own shop or office, or your own church; then with those beyond, with whom you may share yourself and your love for God.

THE
EIGHTH WEEK

The Meditation

FATHER IN HEAVEN, THY STRENGTH IS NOT YET MY STRENGTH, NOR THY peace my peace. In thy mercy thou hast called me to start along the Way, and with rejoicing I am taking my first steps. But I am not ready for the heat of the sun nor the blasts of the storm. Continue, O God, to temper the wind to thy shorn lamb!

Let me not enter into temptation. I am still weak in the Way, and I fear the dangers that mark my path. The enemy is too strong for me, and without thy help I will surely fall. I know myself, and though like Peter of old I would not fall away from my Lord, still I need thy providential care. Until I become stronger in the faith, O God, let thy angels of mercy watch over me.

Yet how can I grow in spirit unless I face the testing that comes through temptation? Thou knowest how impatient I am at times. Why do not others understand what is so clear to me? Why will they not listen when I would tell them of thy love? What makes them so slow to move when I tell them what to do?

Can I learn patience if I am not tempted to impatience? Can I learn to wait before thee if I am not tempted to hurry thee?

I pray sincerely that I may grow in love. Then thou dost cause me to come face to face with one whose personality irritates me or whose past ways make resentments rise. Surely this is entering into temptation! Yet how else may I overcome these faults except that in thy wisdom thou dost lead me into these ways of testing?

Help me, my Father, to greet as pure joy any sort of trial that comes to me, for I know with James that the sterling temper of my faith which produces endurance comes only from thee. (See Jas. 1:2 Moffatt.) So I do not ask that thou remove from me all temptations, O God, but only that thou grant me strength to withstand them, for in thee, and thee alone, is my hope.

"I'm Not to Blame!"

(CONFESSION—1)

The prayer of confession is an awareness of the self in its inadequacy and sin. It is a cry of despair, of humiliation, that admits the sorry truth about oneself.

Seldom do we see this truth because of our relationship to others. We say that we are as good as they are, or perhaps a little better. In comparison with others we bolster our own claims to goodness. How can we call ourselves sinners? What have we done that is any worse than the actions of others—or even as bad? When we look around us on the horizontal level of human relationships we are not apt to make confession of any weaknesses.

Mrs. B, an elderly woman of saintly faith, brought together a dozen women of her church to form a prayer class. The first meditation of their study book, *Two or Three Together*,[1] spoke about one's many selves—I am Anger, I am Fear, I am Pride, and so on.[2] In the period of sharing Mrs. B declared, "We are Christian women who have long served in the church. This meditation hardly applies to us."

Four weeks later, during the sharing time of her class, Mrs. B said, "This past week I have been going over our first meditation about one's

---

[1] *Op. cit.*

[2] See pp. 55-56, of the exercise for The Tenth Week.

name being Legion. I have been checking each one of the selves, and I find that every one of them is mine!"

She did not discover this by looking about her and noting the differences between herself and others. God revealed it to her through his love as she saw herself in relationship to him in the opening weeks of her prayer class.

So it was that Isaiah made his confession: "Woe is me! For I am lost; for I am a man of unclean lips, and I dwell in the midst of a people of unclean lips; for my eyes have seen the King, the Lord of hosts!" (Isa. 6:5.) Was he really so terrible a sinner? Was he an adulterer, a thief, a murderer, a drunkard, or any other of the "popular" sinners of the flesh? Not at all. But Isaiah *saw* the Lord, high and lifted up. In the light of this awful revelation Isaiah knew himself to be a man unclean. His was a subtle sinning, the prides and angers and resentments and condescensions by which he separated himself from others or from his true self or, worst of all, from God. Sin is a barrier raised between ourselves and another, between ourselves and our best selves, or between ourselves and God. Sin is basically disobedience, the refusal, though subtle, to be loving, to be pure, to be faithful, to be truthful.

Years ago a magazine cover pictured a baby boy in a white romper suit sitting on the floor. To his left was an upturned coal scuttle. His hands and face and romper suit were smudged with coal black. Curled up on the boy's right was a black cat, watching the child at play. The child was looking up at his mother, while pointing accusingly at the black cat. The title of the picture was "His First Lie."

How subtly we adults too blame others for our wrongdoing. What a relief it is for some of us to learn through psychoanalysis that we are not really to blame for what we are—it is because of our grandfather's cantankerousness or our elder brother's aggressiveness! It is not our fault!

When we are face to face with the living God, however, we see the truth of ourselves. We admit it first to ourselves, and then in our need, we confess it to him.

Begin then by asking yourself, In the light of my growing understanding of God's love, what am I learning about myself? Do I believe that in any way I merit or deserve the many gifts of his love? Can I merit his love?

> How cometh it to pass
> that into such as me
> Floweth Almighty God,
> into one drop the sea? [3]

Here is the wonder of God's love and God's grace, that in spite of what I am, of what I do, he still gives of himself to me!

Then tell him just what you are finding out about yourself. Do not hold back anything from him, for you cannot deceive him. As each day opens up a new facet of your real self offer that new insight. God does not want only your good qualities, your patience, your loveliness, your kindliness, your self-control. He wants you just as you are, all that you are, your impatience, your unloveliness, your unkindliness, your lack of self-control, as well as the good qualities. Give him everything that you are.

---

[3] Angelus Silesius, *The Cherubinic Wanderer*, tr. Willard R. Trask (New York: Pantheon Books, 1953), p. 30. Used by permission.

THE
NINTH WEEK

The Meditation

GREAT AND GLORIOUS IS MY GOD. IN THE MORNING OF THE WORLD THOU didst bathe the earth with life-bringing waters, and the first seeds rooted and became tenacious plants. They grew and multiplied under thy watchful eye, and in their dying helped form the soils that cover the earth. Through the valleys and upon the hills roamed the animals thou didst create, each with his own kind, and in time man stepped forth in thine own image. All that he saw from the highest hill was thy gift to him.

Even more didst thou give of thy bounty to man. Out of the bowels of the earth he has brought forth coal and oil and the minerals by which he has built his civilization. Long before man dwelt upon the face of the earth thou didst prepare these gifts for him. Through his mind thou didst show man the ways of research by which he might take thy gifts and use them for himself and for generations to come.

Yet thy gifts to man were not finished, for now thou hast opened to him new worlds flung far distant into space. Is there to be no limit to man's reach? Or will he find a greater people, with a God greater than thou art?

How wonderful is man! With giant strides he covers the pathways of the land and the sea and the air. He holds thy whole world in his hands.

Thy world? Yea, Lord, it is thy world, not man's world. It is his only to use. Thou art the sovereign of the universe, and man is but one of thy creatures. *Thou* dost hold the whole world in thy hands—including man! Thou art the eternal God, Creator of all life, Maker of the heavens and the earth, of the world and all worlds.

> And God walked, and where he trod
> His footsteps hollowed the valleys out
> And bulged the mountains up.
>
> Then he stopped and looked and saw
> That the earth was hot and barren.
> So God stepped over to the edge of the world
> And he spat out the seven seas—
> He batted his eyes, and the lightnings flashed—
> He clapped his hands, and the thunders rolled—
> And the waters above the earth came down,
> The cooling waters came down.
>
> Then the green grass sprouted,
> And the little red flowers blossomed,
> The pine tree pointed his finger to the sky,
> And the oak spread out his arms,
> The lakes cuddled down in the hollows of the ground,
> And the rivers ran down to the sea;
> And God smiled again,
> And the rainbow appeared,
> And curled itself around his shoulder.[1]

[1] From *God's Trombones* by James Weldon Johnson. Copyright 1927 by The Viking Press, Inc., 1955 by Grace Nail Johnson. Reprinted by permission of The Viking Press, Inc.

"Who Am I Trying to Impress?"

(CONFESSION—2)

Charles Stinnette of the Department of Psychiatry and Religion at Union Theological Seminary tells of a disturbed mental patient who continually ran himself down. He couldn't do anything; he didn't amount to anything; no one was interested in him; he was less than a cipher. He just could not bear himself. When a counselor suggested to the patient that God cared for him, he quickly responded, "God can't stand me either."

This points to a danger in introspection, that we may become so involved with our own sins and weaknesses, real and imagined, that we become lost in the morass of ourselves. Even God no longer can stand us! If this were solely the comment of a mental patient, it could be quickly passed by. Too many of us, though, have thought in a similar vein. As a result of this dark introspection, there is little health in us.

So the *Book of Common Prayer* speaks the truth: "We have left undone those things which we ought to have done; And we have done those things we ought not to have done; And there is no health in us." Out of such spiritual malaise, Paul cried out: "Who will deliver [us] from this body of death?"

It is not unhealthy to examine ourselves as God by his grace begins to show us to ourselves. It is his gift to us that we can see ourselves as we truly are—if we want to do so.

Mr. S was a business executive who took a personality-rating test along with others in a church discussion group. Together the group studied the ratings, wondering why they revealed what they did. Mr. S said later, "For the first time I began to see myself through the eyes of others, as we examined each other's personality profiles. I must tell someone what I am finding, so I can find help to understand myself."

He went to a minister with a listening ear and poured out his long story. In gist he told this: "As a high-school youngster I refused to play on the school basketball team, where I was required to feed the ball to the captain, a dead shot. So I quit the team and formed one of my own, where I could shoot as I pleased." "We even beat the school team once," he reported with a gleam.

Then he went on to tell how he refused to take orders from others, except direct ones concerning business from his superiors. He would be no one's flunkey, no one's cat's paw. He even objected to comments from his wife concerning possible action. He was going to make up his own mind!

Finally he ended by saying, "I live in a 40,000-dollar home, though according to my salary rating, I should be in a 30,000-dollar one. I drive a Pontiac, where I ought to be driving a Chevrolet." He paused, then asked, "Who am I trying to impress?"

His question was faulty English but sound psychology. Suddenly God had revealed to him through a personality test and group discussion something of the truth about himself. For the first time in his life he sat down to look at himself, to see himself inwardly.

Now consider yourself. Are you dwelling upon yourself and your sinful way solely because no one else is quite as important to you as you? Are you saying with Paul, "I am the foremost of sinners"? As you list your "sins" are you just a little proud that you have so many "nice fat ones" to list?

If you can admit "there is no health in me" as in humble confession you stand before the wonder and glory of God, and if at the same time you seek diligently for the One who can save you from such death, then you will not be lost in the depths of introspection. "If we confess our sins, he is faithful and just, and will forgive our sins and cleanse us from all unrighteousness." (I John 1:9.)

Are your sins those of a moral nature—lust and drunkenness and obesity and vulgarity and the like, acts which you know are wrong, but which you try to hide from others lest you lose your respectability?

Or are they sins of a more subtle and more dangerous kind—prejudice and pride and self-centeredness and resentments, which tear down the inner spirit?

Ask yourself the question Mr. S asked himself: "Who am I trying to impress?" What is it about yourself that you are trying to hide from others, so that you make a false front? What are you afraid others will see? Why do you try to impress others with the clothes you wear, the location of your house, the kind of car you drive, the names you drop, the church you attend, the clubs you join?

Ask yourself, Just who am I?

THE
TENTH WEEK

The Meditation

WHAT A WASTE OF TIME IT IS FOR ME TO SIT IN DISAPPOINTMENT THAT I did not begin earlier to follow thee. How much more I might have done for thee, how much more I might know of thee, how much more I might know myself if only I had turned to thee sooner! But I did not, and vain regret will do me no good. "What if" is so deadening.

Now is the time. What am I doing with the present? Not what have I done, nor what will I do, is the basis of judgment. Thou dost look at me now. Thou dost judge me now.

With thy help I would make mine a disciplined life. I must turn my back on the past, except to learn from it. I must accept the days that are gone, the opportunities that have fled. I must accept myself for what I am now.

Teach me regularity of prayer until its habitual practice is an unconscious act of the will. When there is pleasure in it and I feel the nearness of thy presence I will bless thy name. But help me, O God, when dryness comes and I feel no pleasure, no affection, to persevere in my prayer. Is it pleasure I seek, a feeling, or is it thyself I would have? O God, grant me the feeling of thy affection for me, but if I have no such awareness of pleasurable sensations, still would I hold to thee, still would I pray to thee, still would I serve thee.

Forbid, O God, that I settle down as though I have arrived, complacently believing that regularity alone will be enough. Open my eyes to fresh insights, to new levels of growth, to deeper commitment. I would press on, taking as much from thee as I am ready for, waiting patiently and humbly to receive the more that thou hast for me. In the now I find my life in thee.

Who Am I?

(CONFESSION—3)

Who am I? With that question we ended our exercise for last week. Do we really know who we are? Do we even want to know the truth about ourselves?

Some of us are afraid of what we may find. We already have suspicions about ourselves, a sense of guilt about deeds or thoughts which we would rather hide than bring into the light. It is not that we do not want others to see the truth. We ourselves are not ready to see the truth. We are uncomfortable, but not quite sure what causes our discomfort.

Some of us have no fear whatever. We know who and what we are. With pride or with shame we recognize the truth about ourselves. But are we correct in this judgment about ourselves?

Remember the story of the Pharisee and the tax collector in the parable of Jesus in Luke 18:9-14. The Pharisee, a religious leader trained carefully in his faith, honored for his piety, stood and prayed sincerely, "God, I thank thee that I am not like other men, extortioners, unjust, adulterers, or even like this tax collector. I fast twice a week, I give tithes of all that I get." He believed he was indeed a devout man, that the tax collector was one to be despised.

Strange, but the tax collector believed the same. He would not go forward into the center of the temple court to pray. That was reserved for the pious, like the Pharisee. He stayed far back against the wall and, in despair, beat his breast without lifting his eyes to heaven. "God, be merciful to me a sinner!" he pled.

Both of them were wrong. Oh, they thought they had the correct labels for themselves and for each other, but God was not fooled, even though they fooled themselves. God saw the pride and contempt of the Pharisee. God knew he was a devout man only in outward appearance. God knew the Pharisee's inner heart.

God also saw the humility of the tax collector, who dared not even turn his face, evil face that he thought it was, toward God's heaven. That evil was as much a fallacy as the piety of the Pharisee. God saw the humble heart. God knew the tax collector was a good man. So Jesus said, "This man went down to his house justified rather than the other."

Consider then, Do I really know myself? Is my judgment about myself a correct one? Never mind the other person for the moment. How about me?

Read this meditation carefully.

My name is Legion. I am many persons, instead of one person.

I am Suspicion, sensitive to slights imagined or real, afraid someone is talking about me.

I am Resentment, not liking certain folk, afraid they are trying to put something over on me, trying to take advantage of me.

I am Envy, unable to understand why some people have what I want but don't have.

I am Anger, flaring up at the slightest irritation.

I am Bitterness, complaining at my lot in life, kicking against circumstance.

I am Fear, afraid to try something new, lest I fail; afraid to accept responsibility, lest I can't carry on.

I am Contempt, scorning those who can't move as fast as I do, think as quickly as I do, pray as easily as I do, give as liberally as I do.

I am Greed, holding back for myself more than I need, excusing my stinginess by my small income.

I am Pride, sure of my place, condescending to those "less fortunate."

I am Self, thinking of self, dreaming of self, desiring for self, loving self.[1]

Once a young minister interrupted the reading of those words to declare with delight, "I can think of several people just like that!" He was answered quickly by a simple layman, "I wasn't thinking about others. I was thinking how these fit me." Who were you thinking about when you read those words? Could they mean you?

Do you feel like the man who protested, "Such words are too negative. We'll never get any place talking like that. Let us be more positive. Why not talk about the good things we are, like love and joy and peace?"

Well, why not? Let's try to do what he suggested. Consider this meditation:

My name is Legion. I am many persons, instead of one person.

I am Innocence, believing everything I hear, accepting whatever I am told.

I am Gentleness, never irritated by others, never disturbed by their bad manners, never upset by their noisy ways.

I am Love, always patient, always kind, always helpful.

I am Thoughtfulness, careful of others lest I hurt them by word of deed, watchful that I do not turn them against me.

I am Patience, not pushing others to see the truth that I see, not hurrying others to come to the Light, but content to let God in his own time move within them as he knows best.

I am Self, honoring my true self, respecting my true self, loving my true self.

Which of these is the real me? Am I one or the other? Or am I some of each? Just who am I?

"God created man in his own image, in the image of God he created him." (Gen. 1:27a.)

---

[1] Freer and Hall, op. cit., pp. 86-87. Used by permission of Harper & Brothers.

THE
ELEVENTH WEEK

The Meditation

THANKS BE UNTO THEE, O GOD, FOR THE JOY OF LIVING. THOU HAST MADE full the day, and the night hours speak of thee. In all my doings thou dost surprise me by joy.

Early in the morning thou art with me. In the freshness of the dawning, in the wonder of a new day, in the opportunity for a new beginning, thy spirit touches me. With expectancy I look forward to each event of the day, knowing that thy providence inspires it, thy love undergirds it, thy joy surrounds it.

How fine it is to have work to do! To set the breakfast table in love for my family, to greet the first customer with delight, to watch the children come trooping into the classroom, to share a cheery "Good morning" with folk in the office, to hear the smooth running of a motor after the switch is turned, to open to a clean page for the new day's jottings, to answer the first call! Blessed be thy name, blessed be thy name.

Every creature speaks of thee. With full throat the birds herald the day, and in the hush of the evening they sing their vespers. The playful kitten rolls and tumbles in mock fight until the weary mother clamps it still with her paw. The lying dog stretches in its sleep, a faint bark telling of cats chased in a dream. The scurrying of small feet in the brush gives promise of rabbit or squirrel or chipmunk astir with life. Even the lizards, motionless as they wait for unsuspecting insects, delight the watcher. Thou hast indeed brought forth for man's enjoyment the creatures of field and wood and sky.

In the energy of children, in the flush of youth, in the strength and beauty of young manhood and womanhood, in the steadfastness of middle years, in the serenity of old age, thou art my joy. Not even the discomfort of pain nor the restlessness of lonely years can take from me the radiance of thy presence in the world about me. O God, continue, I pray thee, to be my joy.

Peeling the Onion of the Self

(CONFESSION—4)

Sin is real. We cannot brush it aside lightly. The apostle Paul is no sentimentalist about that. His cry of despair has been echoed through the centuries: "Who will deliver [us] from this body of death?" We try and try and try again, but we cannot in our own power strip ourselves of evil as we would peel an orange.

Through the grace of God I am a perfectionist. By temperament I try to do everything perfectly. But not through his grace have I insisted that others must be perfect. In years past I have been exceedingly critical of others, demanding of them an almost inhuman perfection. No matter what someone said or did, I was critical of him, boasting that I could do better or complaining that he did it so poorly. At times this criticism bothered me, for it certainly was not loving. Then I would try for a time not to condemn others. I would be successful for an hour or two, a day or two, sometimes for almost a week, but not for longer. My inability to achieve perfection within myself found release in criticizing the faults of others. For years I tried and failed, as I leaned on my own resources.

Then through the grace of God I learned to love a little bit, and the more I loved, the less I criticized others. The more I prayed for others, the less I found fault in them. God through his continuing love showed me how to demand more of myself while at the same time demanding less of others. In time he taught me to discipline myself more carefully when others were disciplining themselves carelessly.

With astonishment I suddenly discovered that some weeks had gone by and not once had I been critical of another person. In my own power I had tried to end this evil way of living with others, but I had been unable to overcome it. Through the grace of God, however, as he taught me how to love, I did overcome it. Yet not I, but the Love that was within me.

So, I had peeled the orange, and the old skin was rolled away! But God was not through with me. One day I discovered that the old critical faculty was back again. Examining myself, I found that I was not as loving as I thought I was! Then the truth came to me: Through God's help, to strip myself of evil was not the peeling of an orange. It was the peeling of an onion. When one peels an orange the peeling is removed forever. Not so with me! I am like an onion, that is peeled, then peeled again, then peeled again. Is there no end to the peeling of an onion? I ask myself.

No wonder Paul wanted to know who could save him, for in himself there was no power. Through God's grace, however, like Paul, we can strip ourselves day by day. We may never quite get to the end of the peeling, but at least the old skin can be removed.

Our growing knowledge of ourselves is neither a circle on which we return to the same place, nor a straight line on which we never return to where we have been. Rather, our growing is a spiral. Each day's experience takes us a bit higher than the day before, so that we have that previous experience to help us interpret our new day. Yesterday's patience or impatience, yesterday's love or hate, teach us better to understand today's.

So we come back again and again to our need for patience, our need for tolerance, our need to check our pride. We are never quite ended with these, but because our growing is a spiral, we can see them, understand them, and through God's grace, peel them better each day.

We hesitate to make our confession, to admit our weaknesses to others. Within a prayer class, where love dwells, we may be able to do so; or we may go to a minister, a counselor, a friend whose listening ear will neither approve nor condemn; but if there is no person to whom we may go freely, we can make our confession to God. We can tell him just what we have done or are doing. We will hide nothing from him.

It is not necessary to speak to others. It is necessary that we speak to God, that we hold nothing back from him. He knows before we speak, true enough, but the act of confession clears our own hearts and consciences, making freedom possible through forgiveness.

Look behind your actions to your motives. When you are angry ask yourself why. Is your pride hurt? Does someone think you are not as capable as you think you are? Does someone brush you off as though you are insignificant? Are you tired, the weight of yourself and your woes so heavy that you are easily irritated? Is your anger merely a kickback against those who do not understand what a difficult time you are having as you try to put up with them? Is not your anger caused by you?

When you refuse to accept a task ask yourself why. Are you really so busy that you do not have time for another? Are you lazy? Do you talk a fine spiel, making folk think you are interested in something, and then seek a way out of doing anything about it because basically you do not care at all? Do you want community betterment—if someone else will do the work? Are you content to bask in your own glow while others struggle in darkness?

Go behind your actions when you are proud, prejudiced, condescending, fearful, or condemning. Just why do you act as you do? How much of your action is because of the sin of yourself, your demand for first place? How much of what you do is because "someone must look out for Number One"?

THE
TWELFTH WEEK

The Meditation

FORGIVE ME, O FATHER. I DO NOT MEAN TO BE HOSTILE. I WANT TO LOVE and be loved. Yet hidden feelings of hostility continually rise within me.

Is it jealousy of my fellow worker that upsets me when he gains an honor that I had sought? Truly I do not hold anything against him, for I want him to have all the prestige that can be his. But I wonder why I did not receive like recognition, for am I not as capable as he? Why should I be left out? Dark is the hostility with which I think of him and of those who chose him above me.

My friend gets a salary increase, and I do not. Whether he deserves it is not the point. My concern is that I did not get a similar raise. I do not ask myself what fault of mine prevented such an increase for me. I am irritated that he gained where I did not, even though I am sure that I deserved as much. It is not fair to me.

Forgive me, O God, when I speak disparagingly of one who is elected or appointed to a task in an organization where I have served longer, when I feel that my years of service should be rewarded before these upstarts who have just joined my group get such a high office. I do not mean to be like the elder Brother, but I have worked hard through long years. I should have a fatted calf killed for me, a party thrown in my honor. People are so unfair to me.

Why am I so hostile? Has my pride been touched? Am I thinking too much of myself, of my own need for recognition, for status? Is the competitive drive at home, at work, in society, so important to me that I am letting hostility seep within?

O blessed Lord, teach me to be humble. Teach me to understand the hidden influences at work within myself, that I may know how to handle them through thy grace. Teach me how to overcome the pressures from without which make me seek for myself position and power.

"Whoever would save his life will lose it; and whoever loses his life . . . will find it." (Matt. 16:25.)

Climbing Out of the Abyss Takes Time!

(CONFESSION—5)

How many times have we cried in despair, "I just don't seem to be a bit better now than before I began my search to know God and myself." We have learned about patience, and we have prided ourselves upon our growing practice of that virtue. Then one day we are chagrined to find how impatient we really are. Through the grace of God we are beginning to conquer resentment, and we are pleased with our more gentle spirit. Then we are shocked to find how angry we become over a simple matter. All these weeks and months of prayer and devotion, yet look at us. We are more heathen than before! Why?

Part of the answer is clear enough. We forget that we do not live in a vacuum. Our living is social. Through our early days we take on the coloration of those around us. The prejudices of our parents, their tastes, their principles, their ambitions, their fears, their dreams, become ours. The clipped, sophisticated, hard voice of the ten-year-old is in perfect imitation of his older brother, a hero home from the big city. An elderly woman, world traveled, widely read, confessed that she could not like Abraham Lincoln, even though she knew history did not agree with her. "My grandmother raised me for the first ten years of my life," she said, "and grandma, a Southerner who saw

Yankee raiders lay waste her Tennessee farm home, hated Lincoln and the North. She fed me on her hatred, and I've never been free from it."

We do not become what we are in a moment. Long years of habit shape our thinking and our feeling. We do not realize that we are largely shadows of our culture, with little substance of our own. The mood of our generation, the demand for success, the immorality of our leaders in business and government and society—to say nothing of the field of entertainment, our condoning of vulgarity, our equation of happiness with possession of material goods, our acceptance of prosperity as the gift of the gods, have all had their share in making us what we are now. How then can we expect to change ourselves overnight?

More, the habit of our years of thinking and feeling has been strengthened by the pressures of society upon our action. Wipe away those tears and be a man, we are told. Yet the cleansing of tears is the gift of God, evidence of the tendering of the spirit by a loving God. Stand up and fight back, we teach both our boys and girls. Be proud, don't let anyone walk over you. Assert yourself. Humility is for Casper Milquetoast. So we are afraid to be gentle, lest someone laugh at us; afraid to be patient and conciliatory, lest someone think us soft. Worse yet, we keep quiet in time of social unrest to protect our own interests, not realizing that our silence speaks louder than our words. We shield our better thoughts and feelings from others, until in time they are hidden in our deep unconsciousness. Then we are as brash, as empty, as those around us. Outwardly we are happy, for we have gained social approval; inwardly, we lose the ability to weep with the betraying Peter.

We are not always "happy," however. A high-school lad raised the question: "I worked hard in my classes, and I made good grades. Then the fellows called me a 'brain' and wouldn't have anything to do with me. So I let my grades slump, and they liked me again. But *I* don't like me now. What am I going to do?"

A seminary student came from a conservative background with puritanical overtones. His field work in his first year was with a boys' club in lower Manhattan. For several weeks he remained an outsider, until finally he learned to shoot dice. He reported, embarrassment mixed with pride, "Now I am one of them, and for the first time the program is beginning to move ahead." Compromise does not belong to the black-and-white Puritan, nor to the perfectionist. But a realistic understanding of human nature finally overcame his scruples. In humility he took his place as a sinner with sinners—except that he would not call them sinners any more.

He learned what all of us must face sooner or later: We cannot keep separate our spiritual or religious life from our practical, everyday life. The two must be the same. Either both will be full of self-seeking—the getting of spiritual goods and material goods alike for me, for my interests, for my gain, for my pride; or both will be full of other-seeking, the use of spiritual and material "goods" alike for others and for God. The one who tries to gain the world six days a week and heaven one day soon finds himself in eternal conflict, a religious schizophrenic.

What then to do? First, let us be very patient with our growing— "first the blade, then the ear, then the full grain in the ear." Our habits cannot change overnight. Only the conceited person believes that he is so strong in his spiritual life that his can be a sudden, complete change. His turning from self may be in an instant, but the march along the way must be a struggle. The years of climbing out the abyss of self may equal the number of years spent in climbing down into it. God will show us ledges along the way where we may rest ourselves for a time, and when we are ready he will point out new ones to us. We must wait patiently in the storm until the winds and squalls of self-concern lessen, so we can see ahead once more.

Confess to him your impatience, and accept the speed of his plan.

He will give you clear paths ahead as soon as you are ready for them, but your readiness depends upon your acceptance of yourself and upon your recognition that spiritual change is like physical change. One moving suddenly from darkness to light is blinded. One coming quickly out of the depths of the sea gets "the bends."

Not only is there no high-speed elevator to carry you from self to others, there is no surgery that will change your patterns of thought and emotion instantly. New habits must be formed by daily disciplines consciously practiced until your thoughts are his thoughts, your ways his ways.

This means a revolution for you, a turnabout from self, a new world to enter, as strange, and for many, as forbidding, as the change from jungle to urban life in much of central and southern Africa today. To do this alone is well-nigh impossible. Seek out companions for your journey, and in the encouragement of group effort, be patient and persistent, for there is no other way except that of patience and persistence.

THE
THIRTEENTH WEEK

The Meditation

TO BE ALIVE—TO SEE THE GLORY OF THE SUN AND TO REJOICE IN IT, TO
hear sounds all around me and to be glad, to taste a morning meal and
to say it is good, to smell the freshness of a new day and to be grateful, to feel—just to feel—and then to laugh! What a gift thou hast
handed to me through my senses, O God.

Too often, my Father, I begin a day with jaded spirits, unhappy, depressed, afraid. Life is a burden for me, and with groanings I stretch
myself for the tasks of the day. Then thy spirit touches me—through
the song of a child, the flight of a bird, the scent of a rose—and my
burden is lightened. Once again I see the world about me. Once again
I desire to live.

In the mystery of thy providence, some of us have known physical
suffering in times of illness. Into the depths of darkness we have
gone, caring little at times whether we lived or died—so weak in body,
so numbed with pain, that we were bereft of desire. Then through thy
healing power, O thou divine Physician, renewal came to us. Hope
stirred within as restful sleep returned. Our appetites began to revive,
food tasted like food again, and the normal physical functions of the
body became a pleasant surprise. We rejoiced in thee with great rejoicing, and thy peace comforted us. Just to be alive, physically alive!

How strange and how wonderful is this body of mine! It is thy gift
to me. Forgive me, O God, when I mistreat my body, temple of thy

spirit. Forgive me when I deny its beauty, or condemn its appetites, or chasten its desires. Forgive me when I fail to rejoice in the wonder of the body, in the delight of the senses.

These are thy gifts to me, made holy through thy purposes. Grant, O God, that I may fulfill thy purposes for me through my body.

"It's His Fault, Not Mine!"

(LOVE IN ACTION—2)

"Just look at that bed! No matter what I tell him, he just won't straighten it up. I don't see how he can get it into such a heap!" Mary slumped down on a chair as she sighed. If only Jimmy would pick up his things and straighten his bed as other boys do! Surely no other mother has the trouble with teen-agers that she has with her seventeen-year-old son.

Mary was hurt. Again Jimmy had gone to school in a pout, with her nagging sounding in his ears. Couldn't she get along with her son? He really wasn't a bad boy, but how exasperated she was with him! Was he on his way to becoming a juvenile delinquent? O God, what can I do, was her prayer.

In her morning prayer class she was learning the meaning of love. But what had she learned about loving Jimmy? What good was love for others—and for God—if it did not mean love for Jimmy too?

Mary jumped up. She went to the bed and put all the bedclothes onto a chair. Taking the undersheet, she placed it on the bed, then smoothed it carefully, blessing Jimmy with every brush of her hand. So with the top sheet, the blanket, the spread, with gentle, loving strokes she smoothed each one, praying for Jimmy with thanksgiving and blessing all the while. What a fine boy he really is! And how much she loved him! She left the room in peace, a deep quiet stealing over her spirit.

That afternoon as Jimmy burst into the house after school, he called to his mother, "Hi, Mom!" As she told about it afterwards, she said, "It was the first time in weeks that Jimmy had called out like that. My heart almost broke with love when he did it." Then she added thoughtfully, "May God forgive me for waiting so long to forget myself."

Jimmy is not much different from other teen-agers. Rare is the boy or girl who carefully picks up his room each day. He has far more important things to do—or so he thinks. Mother has to face that uptorn room. With a snap of the sheet and a toss of the blanket, and perhaps a pounding of the pillow, she makes the bed. If she could only lay her hands on him long enough—! Then he comes home after school, drops his books on the kitchen floor as he opens the refrigerator, and Mom gets after him again! When will he ever learn?

George had something of the same kind of problem. He had been employed by his corporation to establish a safety department. For nearly six months he had worked carefully to draw up a plan that would meet every situation throughout the large plant. Now he was ready to present his first complete outline.

Unfortunately, George's immediate superior was one whom George did not like. There was nothing wrong about him; he just seemed to rub George the wrong way. Into the office George went with the completed outline. His colleague liked most of it, but stated that two sections must be changed completely. George argued, but the superior was adamant. "Revise those sections before you go any further," he told George.

In fury George returned to his own office. He slapped the papers down on his desk. Damned if he would go ahead with it! He was the safety specialist, not the other man!

Then George remembered that the night before in his prayer class he had learned that love for God without love for his neighbor was meaningless. Did he love his superior? He did not! But he should—especially if he truly loved God.

So George began to pray about the whole problem. He offered the plans to God. They were the best he could do, and God knew they were just right! Then he began to pray for his superior. After all, he was a pretty good guy. He had worked in the plant for many years, and his interest was the welfare of the men. God bless him and keep him.

George picked up the plans. "Help me to see through his eyes," George prayed. "Maybe he does have a point." So George began to re-read the outline very carefully.

An hour later as George was walking to the water cooler he saw his superior coming down the corridor. "Howdy, George," the man called to him. George was pleased and surprised. Had he not stormed out of that man's office only an hour ago?

A week later George returned with a new outline. He asked for suggestions concerning the two disputed sections, saw the other man's point of view, and the two of them quickly worked out a solution. "He's a pretty fine man to work for," George said later.

What is your problem? How much of it rests upon the other fellow? How much of it depends upon yourself? Where can you put your love into action?

> He drew a circle that shut me out—
> Heretic, rebel, a thing to flout.
> But Love and I had the wit to win:
> We drew a circle that took him in.[1]

[1] Edwin Markham.

THE
FOURTEENTH WEEK

The Meditation

STILL THOU MY HEART, O GOD, THAT I MAY HEAR THY VOICE.

In the name of expediency I have learned through thy help to control my tongue. I am too polite to wrangle, too well mannered to shout, too careful of my reputation with others to speak in anger. Through thy mercy I have learned the first step toward inner quiet as I have gained partial control over my tongue.

My heart is not always still, however. Sometimes I smile outwardly, calm and serene on the surface, while underneath rages a storm of anger and bitterness. Tightly suppressed it is, yet the storm inwardly destroys any semblance of real peace, a maelstrom with no outlet. Its noise hides thy voice; its darkness blots out thy presence. Like Lear of old I am alone, terribly alone, unable to find thee, unable to find surcease, even unable to find myself.

Sometimes it is a slow burning within, resentment gathering its tiny pieces of firewood, pride gradually adding its larger branches, then suddenly, fear tossing on its logs, until the holocaust is a hell within. Would that Lazarus might bring cool water to my parched spirit, but he is not here—and thou art not here.

O forgive me, my God, that though I have learned to control my tongue in part, yet I have not learned to still my heart. It takes so long for me to quiet the storm, to put out the fire. I cannot do this alone, but through thy love and mercy I believe I may find strength to turn from myself and its alarms. With a plea for forgiveness I lift my head to thee. With a cry for thy love I throw myself upon thy mercy. Teach me to be still in heart, that I may know thee, that I may know thou art God, my God.

To Be Lost—Then Found!

(FORGIVENESS—1)

Prayers of forgiveness reveal an awareness of God's pardon. "Woe is me" is our confession, "for I am undone!" But we need not stay in that despair. Through his grace God offers his forgiveness to us. "Then flew one of the seraphim to me, having in his hand a burning coal which he had taken with tongs from the altar. And he touched my mouth, and said: 'Behold, this has touched your lips; your guilt is taken away, and your sin forgiven.'" (Isa. 6:6-7.)

To be lost, and then to be found! Is there any greater joy than that? Pity the man who does not know forgiveness. The radiance of the Christian Church is in proportion to the number of people within its fellowship who have found forgiveness.

One day a young woman came to me. "Perhaps you can help me. I'm living in hell. I want God's forgiveness, but I can't find it. What can I do?"

She then said she had been a receptionist for a doctor. Over a period of almost a year she had taken small sums from cash payments, until it amounted to more than a thousand dollars. Finally the doctor caught her. She had paid back some 700 dollars and had agreed to repay the remainder. Though he had refused to give her a recommendation for a new job—how could he, she wanted to know—she believed all had been worked out satisfactorily with him. She could not, however, find God's forgiveness. In the five months since she had been caught in her theft she had sought release, but could find no help.

Would she ever steal again? Oh, no! She had learned a harsh lesson. Had she made everything right with her doctor? Yes, as far as she could. He was friendly to her and had agreed not to prosecute her. She intended to repay all the stolen money. Was she really sorry about the whole matter? Oh, yes! She would never do anything like that again!

So I told her, "God is a God of love. If you are truly sorry and never intend to do anything like that again, and if you have tried to make amends with the doctor, then all you need to do is to accept God's forgiveness."

"What then?" she wanted to know.

"What then?" I repeated in surprise.

"Yes," she said, "and what then?"

"Oh, you mean, do you have to attend church and read your Bible and pray every day?"

"That's what I mean," she declared. "What bargain do I have to make?"

"None whatever," I told her. "There are no strings attached. God's forgiveness is freely yours, if in repentance you will accept it."

"That's what I've been waiting to hear," she said, and she began to cry. She had been told by several church friends that she must do this or do that to gain God's forgiveness, and she did not believe a bargaining God would forgive her. If he would just take her just as she was, however, lost in her sorrow, determined to make amends, then she could believe.

She did accept his forgiveness, and a quiet joy possessed her. Later she did attend a church, became a member, and joined a prayer class. This came after she found once again the love and forgiveness of God, however.

John says God is love. "If we confess our sins, he is faithful and just, and will forgive our sins and cleanse us from all unrighteousness." (I John 1:9.) He requires no bargaining, no agreement to sign that for his forgiveness we will pay thus and so; nor does he require that we wait on probation, proving our good intention.

In the parable of the two brothers (Luke 15:11-32) Jesus tells that when the prodigal came home the father immediately took him into the family, with a ring for his finger, shoes for his feet. So, Jesus would suggest, is the love of God for us. On the other hand, the teachings of Buddha have a similar parable about a lost son. In this one the father does not reveal himself to the boy until "after many years," during which the son has proved himself worthy to be called "son."

It is not your worth or my worth that wins forgiveness. Only through the worth of God, the love of God, does forgiveness come. Because he is love, by his very nature he cannot help himself. He will not turn his back upon us, but we turn our backs upon him. When once again we turn toward him, like the father of the prodigal son he comes running to receive us to himself.

Have you done something wrong, for which you seek forgiveness? Have you forgiven yourself, accepting yourself for what you are? Or are you whipping yourself in horror, afraid that God requires severe punishment in his justice? Once a mother scolded her young son, then told him: "Now tell God how bad you are!" He responded, "You tell him. He's not speaking to me!"

God is speaking to you. Are you speaking to him? His forgiveness is yours for the asking.

When he had finished he examined himself how he had discharged his duty; if he found *well,* he returned thanks to God; if otherwise, he asked pardon; and without being discouraged, he set his mind right again, and continued his exercise of the *Presence* of God, as if he had never deviated from it. "Thus," said he, "by rising after my falls, and by frequently renewed acts of faith and love, I am come to a state wherein it would be as difficult for me not to think of God as it was at first to accustom myself to it."

So wrote Brother Lawrence in his true simplicity.

THE
FIFTEENTH WEEK

The Meditation

STRANGE IS THE WORKING OF THY PROVIDENCE. HOW DOES IT HAPPEN THAT two seemingly isolated events through the catalyst of thy spirit bring together two people? A couple with a son moves into a neighborhood about the time another couple with a daughter moves there—and boy meets girl! A youth chooses a college and finds there a teacher unknown to him previously—and a new horizon is opened for the student. A woman receives a printed announcement of a class, and attending the session, hears a speaker whose influence changes her entire outlook on life.

At the moment of meeting no one knew thy spirit was at work, O God. Not until long afterwards did I recognize that events are not unrelated events. Thou didst bring them together in thy wisdom, and I received the benefit of thy providence. Thanks be unto thee for thy guiding hand.

As I look back through the years, I see incident after incident that reveal thy purpose for me. A book came into my hands, and the direction of my life changed. A letter written to a stranger opened doors into a new world. A visitor speaking in my church brought renewal of my faith and the determination to seek thee with the whole heart and the whole mind. A new job—besides bringing a new home, a new church, and new friends—offered a new chance to serve thee with deeper commitment.

How can I thank thee, Father, for thy providence through the days of my years? In a manner that I cannot understand thou hast directed my comings and my goings. I thank thee that I have been alert enough to follow thee, even when I did not know it was thy hand that was directing me.

Thy thoughts have not always been my thoughts, and thy ways have not always been my ways. Yet thou hast continued to lead me, to bless me, to love me, yea, even to trust me. May I be worthy of thy love and thy trust, O Father, as humbly I seek to know thy thoughts, to follow thy ways, to co-operate with thy providence.

Restoring a Right Relationship

(FORGIVENESS—2)

Create in me a clean heart, O God,
and put a new and right spirit within me. (Ps. 51:10.)

Here is the twofold act of forgiveness—the cleansing of the heart and the restoring of right relationships.

When I sin I break a right relationship. I raise a barrier between myself and another. My friend says something to me, and in anger I call him a fool. He would reach out to me in love, but I turn from him. My anger grows into fierce resentment, dirtying my heart. Then one day I recognize my wrongdoing and turn toward him. "I'm sorry," I say, "please forgive me." Because he is a loving person, he answers me, "Oh, that's all right. I'd forgotten all about it!" We grasp each other's hands, and once again our right relationship is restored.

Sometimes an apology is necessary—not that our friend will require it, but we need it, a sign of our own sorrow, of our intention to restore a broken fellowship. If we refuse an apology, then we are not sorry, we do not intend to cement a friendship. We are but insisting on having our own way. "He should give in, but I'll not do so!" There can be no forgiveness when either person is self-demanding.

Sometimes restitution is necessary. We return the stolen money, repair the broken window, or even go to jail. Our act, as far as within us lies, shows our good faith—that we do wish to restore the right relationship that we have lost.

We cannot always make amends, however. Perhaps a child is killed or a man is permanently disabled because of our unintentional carelessness. No matter what we may do in seeking forgiveness, we cannot alter the circumstances. A man whom we have injured with sharp tongue may move away before we can go to him. A woman may die, and when in later years we seek for her to ask forgiveness for a wrong, we find she is dead. Then we can only do what is possible for the living. We may offer our wrongdoing to God, that his forgiveness may be ours. Though our regret will remain ever with us, it will not be a malignant sore.

Fortunately, most of us have opportunity to seek forgiveness. Years ago in frustration I spoke angrily to a friend. I moved from his community to a distant place. Three years later I saw a man who looked much like my friend. The shock of similarity brought awareness of my continuing separation from him. The next day I wrote a letter of apology to him, telling him how foolish I had been and how unnecessary had been my anger. Within a week he replied, extending his forgiveness and friendship to me. Though I never saw him again, for he died shortly afterwards, God through his grace had led me to write a letter that restored once again a right relationship.

This must be said: It is never quite the same relationship again on human levels. The doctor, though forgiving, will always remember that a nurse stole from him. He cannot give her a recommendation for another position. She cannot start anew as though nothing had happened.

So it was with the return of the prodigal in Jesus' parable about the two sons. His father did order a ring for his finger and shoes for his feet. His son who had been lost was found. But the boy did not have any more inheritance; he had to go to work for a living; nor could he remove the years of hurt that weighed upon his father. Perhaps for most of us our deepest regret is, though once again love can restore a right relationship, it can never remove the years of hurt. If only we might replace them—but we cannot.

It is the same with the forgiveness of God. Though we may know the cleansing of our hearts, and though we may once more know the intimacy of fellowship with the loving Father, we can never quite remove from our minds the sin that has been ours. We do not ponder upon it; certainly we do not gloat over it—how many have been "proud" that they had been such sinners in their youth. Normally we put it away from our thinking, but in humility we know what we have been, and we know what we are. Yet we know his love and forgiveness, and in gratitude we offer ourselves in service to him.

Paul wrote: "Not that I have already obtained this or am already perfect; but I press on to make it my own, because Christ Jesus has made me his own. Brethren, I do not consider that I have made it my own; but one thing I do, forgetting what lies behind and straining forward to what lies ahead, I press on toward the goal for the prize of the upward call of God in Christ Jesus." (Phil. 3:12-14.)

Perhaps you have been estranged from someone for many years. If he is near at hand go to him, tell him of your new love for God and beg his forgiveness. If he does offer his forgiveness, rejoice with him. If he does not, do not bother him again, but remember him lovingly in your prayers.

Perhaps you need to write a letter, make a phone call, or take a trip to let someone know that you are sorry for what you did. You may need to make restitution for a wrong of years before—or of last week.

Seek the forgiveness of those whom you have wronged, then come with your prayer of forgiveness to God.

> Who shall ascend the hill of the Lord?
> And who shall stand in his holy place?
> He who has clean hands and a pure heart. (Ps. 24:3-4.)

Accept his love, and know the blessing of the Father.

THE
SIXTEENTH WEEK

The Meditation

BECAUSE THOU ART GIVING SO MUCH TO ME, MY GOD, I WOULD THAT OTHERS too might have what I am learning. Thou dost mean so much to me. My day is brighter, my work is easier. Through thy word in Scriptures and in devotional classics I am seeing truths long hidden by my obtuseness. In the worship of the gathered fellowship in my church, I am finding vitality not known to me previously. With those who share in my search for thee I am finding companionship I had not realized could be possible.

No wonder that my zeal that others too should know thee as I am knowing thee grows increasingly strong. I can hardly wait until they too begin attending church as faithfully as I do, that they may know what I am learning. O God, make them listen to thee, make them come to thee. Then they will know for themselves the wonderful joy of serving thee.

Am I really trying to help others—or trying to reform others? Forgive me, O God, when I fall into the temptation to reform others, to change their patterns of life into mine.

I would show them the truth that has been revealed to me. But am I sure that I do know the truth? Have I just begun to learn, so that mine is the half-truth so dangerous to force upon others?

I would compel them to love thee as I love thee. But what do I know about love? Am I trying to reform them, to reshape them into my likeness, as though I now am love? If thou art truly love, wilt thou ever force anyone, compelling him to serve thee, to love thee? Yet here am I, trying to use thee as the leverage to move a friend closer to thee, trying to use thee as a policeman to "make" them do what I believe is best for them.

Father, forgive me when I am unloving in my judgment, impatient in my criticism, scornful in my attitude toward those not following thee as I would follow thee. Is it that in my zeal to reform others I am forgetting my own need to reform? O God, in thy mercy, reform thy people—beginning with me!

Surprised by His Mercy

(FORGIVENESS—3)

Mrs. Jay looked through her third-floor kitchen window down into the drying yard of the apartment house. "Why!" she exclaimed. "Mrs. Brown's sheets and linens are yellow with spots! I can't have that! People will think those are mine!" So she hurried down the back stairs to protest. When she rushed out into the yard, she stopped quickly. The clothes were white as could be! "But I thought—," she started to say to herself. Puzzled, she turned slowly and climbed back to her apartment.

She went to her kitchen window to look below. The spots were there again, but to her embarrassment she saw they were on her own window. "Oh, my," she said, then went to work to clean it.

Forgiveness is ours only when we will assume responsibility for what we are. As long as we alibi or blame another we cannot be forgiven. "It is my fault, my own most grievous fault" is much more than a prayer book phrase. It is the beginning of self-acceptance by which forgiveness may be ours. "This is what I am. I don't like it, and I would prefer to hide it, but I must not. To evade my responsibility is to be arrogant, conceited, sinful. To say 'It isn't my fault' or 'I wouldn't do a thing like that' sets me apart from others. It makes me holier than thou. I am what I am, and with your help, I think I can be a better person. Please forgive me."

Such a prayer will do two things. First, it will put us back into the human race—no longer are we perfectionists who can do no wrong, no longer are we Pharisees who pull our skirts around us lest they be contaminated by the filth of lesser folk. We too are sinners. We are not good. Only One is good. We too stand in need of mercy's help. No matter what the condition of another person we do not reach down a hand to lift him up to us; we look him straight in the eye and say, "Brother!"

We do not judge another. We judge ourselves—but not by others. We judge now only by the grace and mercy of God, the wisdom and mercy of the Eternal, the justice and righteousness of the Holy One. In his sight the good man and the bad man are almost one. Both of us, we believe most fortunately, are his sons.

No wonder, then, we cry out for forgiveness! Unless he pardons us, there is no hope and no joy, only the hell of self with all its guilt and sin. Through his pardon we are made clean; through his love we are restored to fellowship with him and with mankind.

Yes, a prayer of forgiveness does put us back into the human race. Second, it makes it possible for us to forgive others. We know the release that comes through pardon. We know the blessed relief of restored fellowship. We are ready to reach out with forgiving hand to others.

As far as lies within us we will do everything possible to forgive others. We can hardly go to others and say, "I want to forgive you." That would make unrepentant folk say we are condemning them further, calling them sinners by implication. We must wait until they come to us.

We must be watching, keeping the doors open for their possible coming, looking from the housetop for the return of the wanderer.

Then we should never say upon their return, "It's about time you came back" or "I thought you would never come." We should welcome them as though nothing had happened, except that we had missed them. This is not to ease their embarrassment in seeking forgiveness; though that may happen. It is to let them know that we do love them, that we are happy to be one with them in fellowship again.

In Luke 7:36 ff Jesus ate dinner with Simon, a Pharisee. A certain woman came in love and poured ointment over the feet of Jesus. To Simon Jesus spoke of the woman: "You gave me no kiss, but from the time I came in she has not ceased to kiss my feet. You did not anoint my head with oil, but she has anointed my feet with ointment. Therefore I tell you, her sins, which were many, are forgiven, for she loved much; but he who is forgiven little, loves little." (Vss. 45-47.)

Important is the last phrase: "He who is forgiven little, loves little." Our forgiveness of others will be in proportion to our own forgiveness by God. When in my arrogance and pride I seek but little forgiveness, I cannot forgive much in others. When I come in total repentance, however, accepting fully the love of God through his pardon, then I can reach out in full love and pardon to others. As I have received his mercy so I grant his mercy. My niggardliness in forgiving others or my generosity toward others is a measure of my own acceptance of God's forgiveness.

As a consequence of my acceptance of his forgiveness, I find it very difficult to condemn others. Once that was not so. But his love has removed the need to condemn. It no longer is necessary for me to build myself up by tearing down others. I am not that important to me, now that he has permitted me to return to the human race. I can only sympathize with others, understanding full well that if I had been in their shoes, I would probably have been much worse in thought and action. How, then, can I fail to forgive, knowing myself as well as I do, and knowing him even as little as I do?

Consider your own forgiveness. How do you come to the loving

Father? Is it quietly "by night" as Nicodemus came to Jesus, not sure what you will find, not sure how much you will permit God to forgive you? Yet you come, ready to receive, ready to be taught, ready to be loved and to love. Do you come like the woman with the ointment, not really expecting forgiveness, hardly daring to ask for it, but knowing your need to love him, to serve him? How God does then surprise you with his mercy, as he declares, "Your sins are forgiven."

Perhaps you come like Zacchaeus, bored with your life, lonely as an outcast from religion and society, with no meaning to your days, suddenly to find yourself accepted by God, sitting down at his table in joyous feasting. No wonder you offer restitution for any fraud, any deceit, adding to this the sharing of yourself with others. You may come like Saul of Tarsus, breathing fire and vengeance in your zeal, setting yourself up as an instrument of iron in the hand of a God of wrath. Then a light shines upon you; his mercy melts the steel of your heart; and you go down on your knees to become a humble instrument in his hands, to be molded by him into a vessel from which his love may be poured in never-ending flow.

However you may come, know this: In direct proportion to your acceptance of God's forgiveness is your ability to forgive.

THE
SEVENTEENTH WEEK

The Meditation

THOU DIDST TOUCH THE EYES OF A MAN BLIND FROM BIRTH, AND HE SAW! What surprise, what puzzlement, what delight as he looked upon the world about him! Did he still feel his way along known paths, not sure of the new? Was he afraid to move quickly and freely? Did he close his eyes to make certain his way as hands reached out in the bright sun? What did he first wish to see? Whose face did he first seek out?

O God, thou hast opened my eyes, and for the first time I see inwardly. The world is strange and clean, the colors bright, the outlines sharp. Will I need to stumble in old and trusted paths, afraid to step forth into thy new world revealed to me? What now will my eyes long to see?

Like the paralytic of old, suddenly forgiven, and suddenly healed, I too have regained my strength. With shouts and leaps of inward joy I have run off to places where I have not walked before. The bonds of self have been broken through thy mercy, and my new freedom is an unrestrained delight. But old, unused muscles are stiff and sore, and cautiously I hesitate to stretch them into pain. Now I can go alone, where before I needed the help of others; but can I endure the inner solitude with its self-examination, its self-understanding? Forgive me, O God, if I am afraid to be alone, if I hurry to seek others to quiet my inner fears.

Once thou didst touch the ears of a deaf man, and the sound of unheard music surprised him. O God, be praised, thou hast touched my inner ears, and I hear the morning stars singing together and all the sons of God shouting for joy. No longer do I live within myself alone, but "the still, sad music of humanity" breaks upon me. Will I seek out new tones, new harmonies? Or will I prefer the silence that does not disturb?

Thou hast given me new life for old. Faith and hope and love are restored. Teach me, O God, to use for others and for thee, not for myself alone, these gifts of thy spirit.

Meeting Immediate and Long-Range Needs

(LOVE IN ACTION—3)

Jesus gave one command: "Love one another." Evidently the early church obeyed this command, for Tertullian, writing in the third century, quotes the comments of pagans who observed, "See how these Christians love one another."

Today this love may be expressed in one of two ways through personal and group action: In answering either the immediate private need or the long-range social need of individuals and society.

First is the common helpfulness of any decent man who stops to raise up the fallen. Because he is a Christian in truth, he also seeks out those in need, not limiting his aid to those of any one class, creed, color, or nation.

Are there old people living alone in your community whose loneliness you might lighten? Is there a home for the aged near you which would enjoy an occasional party, with a home movie, colored slides, or some good recordings? Do you know a shut-in whom you might surprise and please with a visit? Your minister will give you the names of such folk.

Volunteer for work with the Red Cross, a hospital or nursing home, a settlement house, a community playground, a children's home. Many girls would like to know how to knit or crochet or embroider. Many boys would like an outing for a Saturday.

Find work for an unemployed person, seeing that he receives a loan—not a gift—for necessary transportation or clothing for his job until the next pay day. Arrange credit for him that he may meet living expenses for his family until his bills are caught up. You may wish to share with others in bringing a refugee family to your community, undergirding them financially for the few months needful to establish their home.

Perhaps you will be a baby sitter for a young couple with little income so they may attend a church gathering, a gift deeply appreciated. You may even offer to baby sit while they attend an occasional movie or party.

With others you may seek to refurnish a family burned out, to take turns preparing meals for a family whose mother is in the hospital, or to plant an injured neighbor's garden. You may share in an emergency appeal for flood relief or the like, for folk close at hand or for those in distant places.

Many are the ways your love may reach out to answer the immediate needs of individuals and groups when with imagination you look around you. There is no end to the opportunities God offers by which you may help others.

There are also the long-range social programs. Begin with simple ventures if need be, sharing in community improvement clubs, leagues of women voters, parent-teacher associations. Sponsor the entertainment of foreign students from a college or university in your home and the homes of others for a holiday week end or Christmas or Easter vacation.

Become active in a peace organization, a trade union, or a chamber of commerce, giving yourself as best you can to that one specific interest. Share in a great books discussion group or in another adult education project through which men and women of diversified backgrounds may come together in serious discussion.

Perhaps you might join some others in sponsoring and conducting an espresso house near a large college campus, where students may ask intelligent questions about life and love and faith in a background of sympathetic understanding of today's vocabulary and mores. How fine it would be for a church to offer a social room for occasional meetings for lonely men and women in the rooming-house area of a city!

What can you do to assist in the recreational facilities in a slum area? To help with a scout program in your small town? To sponsor a bookmobile in a rural county? To encourage a mental health program in your community?

Would you be able to give time and money with others to develop a retreat center in your community—either a prayer house for day or evening meetings, or a building large enough to house small groups for two or three days, or even for a week of intensive study? Would you be willing to share in housekeeping, in gardening, in building maintenance, as well as in classes, lectures, and retreats?

Again, there is no limit to the outreach of your love, not even in just beginning to answer the long-range social needs of individuals and society if with imagination and thought you seek to put your love into action.

THE
EIGHTEENTH WEEK

The Meditation

IN THE DAWN OF MY SPIRITUAL LIFE, O FATHER, WHEN FIRST I CAME TO thee with disciplined prayer, thou didst warm my heart with thy love. To pray to thee with simple devotion and to know thy response to my prayer—what a wonderful feeling swept over my whole being! In those beginning days an excitement filled each hour, as I learned to know thee and to know myself. Not because another spoke of thee, but because I knew thee, I came unto thee.

Then the routine days began, with their discipline sometimes broken, their enthusiasm often lessened, their thrill frequently missing. What had happened to me? Had I lost the power to win thy response to my prayer? Did I not pray hard enough? What was my fault?

Forgive me, O God, if ever I think that my prayer merits thy response. Forgive me if I believe that through my doings thy love comes to me. Yet I came very close to blaming thee for the leveling off of my spiritual life. Had I not done all that I should do? Was it not now up to thee? I was puzzled, for surely I had performed all the necessary requirements to grow in prayer. What more could I do?

In thy mercy thou dost hold me at arm's length, lest I run foolishly into thy presence, demanding an audience with thee. Thou knowest my secret pride in my "advancement" in thy kingdom. Thou also knowest, O God, how far from thee I am! Just because I have had "a wonderful feeling," just because thy love didst warm my heart, I thought I had found thee in complete oneness of spirit. Truly I and my Father are one!

We are not, for I am not ready to be one with thee. I do not come to thee in humble commitment. I do not put myself, my pride, my will, my desires behind me. Yet thou art ready for me, waiting in thy love for me to turn to thee. Open my mind and heart to see, O God, that when I forget myself, when I turn from my own selfish thoughts, when I turn from my own self-love, thou dost receive me unto thyself. With trust and in love I throw myself upon thy mercy. Take me into thy heart as thou wilt.

The High Point of Christian Service

(INTERCESSION—1)

In these past few weeks we have been concerned largely with love from God. Aware of his bounty and love to us, we have turned to him with prayers of thanksgiving and gratitude. Aware of the truth of ourselves as he in his love has revealed this to us, we have come to him with prayers of confession. Aware of the pardon that we have received through his love, we have sought cleansing through prayers of forgiveness. We do not leave these three ways of praying behind us now, for they ever should be with us, but now we press on to prayers that reveal our love for God.

Our first set of three prayers had elements of self-interest. We could not avoid this, for self is at the center of our living. We thanked him for what he had done for us. We confessed to him because of our need to place before him our sin. We sought pardon through forgiveness that we might be clean once again, restored to fellowship with him. Though self-interest is at the heart of these prayers, on the whole it is an enlightened self-interest. The "I" and the "me" are there; we must not forget that; but not just for the sake of self alone. We learn to pray that the self may grow in understanding of the self in

91

relationship to others and to God. We learn to pray that we may have fellowship with him not for the self alone but for others—and in time, solely for God. Our prayer is enlightened self-interest as we seek to grow in the life of prayer.

In the three ways of praying to which we now turn our prayer is almost free of self-interest. The prayer of intercession is thinking almost wholly of others. The prayer of adoration is glorifying God for himself alone. The prayer of commitment is the free offering of the self to God in love and service.

First, then, the prayer of intercession, which is an awareness of the needs of others which we offer to God in love. From the beginning of our study we have practiced this prayer of love. We have been praying each day for those on our list, members of our class, members of our family, friends, neighbors, and others for whom we have been concerned. Likewise each day we have been praying for the minister and congregation of our church as they come together in gathered fellowship on the Sunday next. Those of us who are members of a prayer class have also been praying in each class session for special concerns as these have been brought to our weekly session. Already we have been learning through practice something of the meaning of the prayer of intercession.

Because our hearts are full with the love of God, which he has so unstintedly given to us, we cannot help sharing it with others. So we bring others to him, to rejoice with them, or to sorrow with them in their need. We have found in him our Light and our Love. They too may find in him the answer to their need, as we offer them in love to him through our intercession.

This is the high point of Christian service. It is the foundation of all true Christian social action. We do not help another just because he is in need. Any gentleman would do that. We do not help another because it is our duty. Any moralist would do that. We help because we have been helped. We love because he first loved us. We intercede for another because he is our brother, child of the same Father. In love to God we bring our brother in his need to him.

This does not mean that we refuse to do our share in meeting our brother's need. We do all that we can possibly do, but at the same time, we supplement that action with intercession, offering both our brother and our work for him to God.

Fred was a young undertaker. His calls took him frequently into country roads where mud was heavy or where snow was deep. In group conversation one day I said that prayer was putting a shoulder to a wheel and giving a push. Fred objected. "That is not prayer," he declared. "Prayer is saying words."

"All right, Fred," I told him. "The next time I find you stuck in the mud with your ambulance, I'll pray for you while you push."

"Now, hold on!" Fred remonstrated.

The prayer of intercession is a prayer of love. Love gets behind the wheel, pushing with all its might. Love prays in its work and works in its prayer.

You have prayed for others on your list. Have you then gone to them to help them where you could? Your neighbor was sick, and you prayed. Did you then do her laundry or clean her house or prepare a meal for her family? Charley received a thousand yew seedlings. When they arrived he was in bed with an illness that would keep him there for another two weeks. Ray prayed for him, then called a friend, and the two of them planted the seedlings. Have you done the same thing?

Though Floy had joined the church when her husband did, she seldom attended. One fall she enrolled in a prayer class. Day after day with the others she prayed regularly for her minister and the congregation. Then she began attending faithfully. "I had to go to church," she reported, "to see what God was doing there!" Are you attending the church for which you pray?

Perhaps the one for whom you pray lives at a distance. Write him a note, letting him know that you are praying for him, offering him to God in love. Ask him if there is another way by which you may add to that help.

If it is impossible to help further one for whom you are praying, continue your prayer. Undergird him with love faithfully until such time as God may lead you to stop praying.

With imagination and in compassion offer your prayers of intercession. Then, as far as in you lies, be to God his hands and feet in your ministry of love.

THE
NINETEENTH WEEK

The Meditation

THOU HAST PROMISED IN THY MERCY, O GOD, THAT THE POWER OF THY holy spirit will fall upon thy children who wait for thee. Here am I, waiting before thee. Let thy spirit come.

If I seek thy power because of the good that might come to me, forgive me, O blessed Lord. Deep within me I know that through thy power I may do wondrous things, becoming a healer of the spirits of men, an interpreter of thy word, a prophet of thy mysteries, or a teacher of thy way. Only through thy spirit may my prayer be the effectual, fervent prayer of a truly righteous man. I would not gain thy power that it may be mine alone, a thing to handle for my own desire. Keep me from ever trying to use thee or thy gifts just for me, for the enrichment of my personality, for the enhancement of my prestige.

Yet if I seek thy power because of the good that might come to thee, bless me, O gracious Lord. What I can do I would do for thee. What abilities I have I would turn over for thy use, and if through the workings of thy providence thy power should descend upon me so that I am forgotten and thou art known, grant that I may be grateful to be thy instrument.

Come, Holy Spirit, come!
Come as the fire and burn,

Come as the wind and cleanse,
Come as the light and reveal.
Convict, convert, consecrate,
Until I am wholly thine!

Offering the Self for Others

(INTERCESSION—2)

Colonel J is a devoted Christian, active in his church, a leader in community affairs, always called upon by those who seek help in new ventures. He gives most generously both of his time and his money. One day he accepted an invitation to share with other leaders of his Texas city in planning for a boys' work program to help combat juvenile delinquency. The acting chairman asked Colonel J to lead the group in prayer.

"No," the colonel said. "If I pray about this, God will tell me something to do, and I already have more to do now than I can handle properly."

The colonel was correct. An honest prayer of intercession cannot stop with words. It is the foundation stone upon which Christian social action is laid. When one prays for insight into the problem of juvenile delinquency, for the help of God in beginning a boys' work program, or for the raising up of leadership for racial brotherhood, he offers himself in love as he presents to God the needs of others. Hence, he will find time for the action necessary to implement his prayer. He does not "pass the buck" to God, saying to him, "Here is the problem; now you solve it." He works in co-operation with God, knowing that this is his reasonable service.

Colonel J already knows this. For many years he has prayed for someone or for some group, then he has gone into action to co-operate with God as far as he is able in meeting the needs of those for whom he prayed. Here is prayer that is love—The offering of self for others.

Is not the purpose of these exercises in mental prayer to help us know God—To be one with him? Are we not to love him with all our hearts and souls and minds and strength?

Yes, that is so, and this kind of prayer is the first step on that way. The prayers of thanksgiving and confession and forgiveness make us aware of love *from* God. The prayer of intercession is the first of the prayers that make us aware of our love *to* God. Now we forget ourselves, and in forgetting the self and its concerns for itself, we turn in love to God for others. Martin Buber has said, "He who loves brings God and the world together." This is the love of the Cross, the suffering that reaches out with one hand to God and with the other hand to the world.

An unknown Persian poet of centuries ago found this same thing:

> No one could tell me what my soul might be;
> I searched for God, and God eluded me;
> I sought my brother out, and found all three,
> My soul, my God, and all humanity.

So the old Hasidic legends of the Jewish people interpreted the love of one's neighbor as the fulfillment of one's search for God; one such legend has God saying, "You think I am far away from you, but in your love for your neighbor you will find me; not in his love for you but in yours for him."

Through the centuries the greatest of saints have been those who combined the contemplative life with the active—the union of the Mary of the Transfigured Face with the Martha of the Horny Hands, in the phrase of Thomas Kelly. The Desert Fathers, Catherine of Siena, Catherine of Genoa, Francis de Sales, and many others gave themselves in total offering to God through prayer and then went to work for him in active service.

Consider two modern saints of the Protestant faith. Evelyn Underhill, interpreter of mystical prayer, retreat leader, and counselor in the life of prayer, gave time regularly when she was at home in London to working with the poor people of a specific slum area, a complement to her prayer for them. Thomas Kelly, Quaker author of the modern spiritual classic *A Testament of Devotion,* gave himself to racial justice. Each felt it necessary to pray and to work, but neither scattered his work; each chose a particular area and worked diligently in that field.

Let us continue to pray for many causes and concerns, as well as for many individuals, but let us choose carefully the one or two fields in which we can concentrate our effort with God's help. As time permits, let us give of ourselves in other ways too, just so we do not scatter ourselves; then our lives will be lives of true prayer.

When you pray for peace for the peoples of the world do not lose yourself in generalities. Be specific, upholding a congressman, a senator, the President of the United States, a world leader in some specific action. Then write to him, telling him of your prayer, giving him your encouragement. Most letters to public officials are condemnatory, offering criticism rather than commendation. A man can work much better when he knows another is praying for him and encouraging him.

Be honest with yourself. Do not pray for something for which you cannot or will not help. Bea told in her prayer class that she had received an announcement about children from an inner-city parish who sought a week or two in a country home. "I would be very glad to have two girls from the parish to be with my two daughters for a month this summer—but they might be Negro children, and I just can't accept that as yet. It would be wrong for me to ask only for white girls, and I know it's wrong for me to be prejudiced. Some day I may grow out of my prejudice, but not yet," she said. So she was willing to give some money to help the summer project, but she could not pray for it. Not until she would be willing to give herself wholly to its program.

What project do you shy away from, lest you find yourself in a ticklish situation? Where does your love reach a limit beyond which you cannot at the moment go? Are you unable to join in prayers for an enemy leader, for a member of another social class, racial group, or political party? Do you refuse to pray for a Jew, a Roman Catholic, a Negro, a white man, an Oriental?

What are you willing to do, God being your helper, about this inability to pray in love for others?

THE
TWENTIETH WEEK

The Meditation

FATHER, FORGIVE ME FOR MY IGNORANCE OF THE MEANING OF WORDS. What the dictionary teaches is not enough for me, for definitions and illustrations fail to make possible true communication between me and others.

How can I "see" thee? How can I "hear" thee speak? How can I "know" thee? What lies behind these simple words, words so clear, and yet so mystifying?

I can see things, objects, persons, measuring them with my eye. They have shape, size, form, color, which I can describe quite accurately in terms popularly understood.

I can also "see" beauty. What do I "see"? Colors that contrast or blend, patterns that please, forms in light and darkness, mosaics, voids, and how much more. What makes a tree beautiful to me? A poem? A picture? What is the beauty I see in the face of a friend? In the face of the one I love? Do I "see" God in the same way, through relationships, patterns, voids, not with spatial or sensual lines or markings, but through values? How is it, O thou eternal one, that I may "see" thee with my inner eye? For see thee I do!

So I hear tones and overtones, sounds, noises loud and soft. I can measure their volume, their intensity, their vibrations.

Yet I can "feel" the color of tones—harsh or gentle. Some please me, some frighten me, some annoy me. Why does one hymn tune seem beautiful to me and not another? Why does a folk tune appeal to me emotionally, one through patriotism, another through religious fervor, still another through romance? Do I "hear" God in similar fashion, through harmonies, discords, sounds, remembrances? Would that I might hear thee, O God, with the naked ear!

Yes, I know things, objects, persons, even ideas. I am willing to fight at times for my convictions, even to die. I argue; I discuss; I affirm; I deny. They are real to me, and I believe my testimony true. Have I not handled them, heard them, tasted them, known them? "Known" them? How can I "know" ideas? Yet I do say with John of old, "That which was from the beginning, which we have heard, which we have seen with our eyes, which we have looked upon and touched with our hands, concerning the Word of life . . . that which we have seen and heard we proclaim also to you, so that you may have fellowship with us." (I John 1:1-3.)

O God, my God, forgive the barriers I raise between myself and thee, between myself and others, through the use and misuse of words, symbols, implications, connotations. Deep within my inner self thy spirit moves, with judgment, with conviction, with love. Help me to understand thyself in spite of the poverty of words. Help me to know the Reality that lies behind these symbols. Grant that I may know thee, the only true God, and Jesus Christ whom thou hast sent.

The Priestly Office of the Christian

(INTERCESSION—3)

Arthur J. Gossip, English teacher of prayer, wrote that intercession is the priestly office of the Christian. The true priest intercedes before his God for his people, bringing their needs to him in supplication and praise. As Protestants we do not believe that we need a priest especially ordained to stand between us and God, for we believe with

Luther in the priesthood of all believers. Hence, each one of us is a priest, whose high privilege it is to make an offering of love for others to God through our intercession.

God has done great things for us. He had blessed us, loved us, and kept us in the hollow of his hand. In our love and joy for what he has done for us, we bring to him a friend in need. Surely he will bless our friend too! So intercession always becomes part of the prayer life of a thankful heart, a growing heart, a heart reaching out beyond itself to God and man.

Here is the source of evangelism: Look what happened to me! I must share God's love to me with another. So I pray to God for this other, then search him out to tell him of the wonder and mercy of God the Father. So Daniel T. Niles rightly defines evangelism as one beggar telling another beggar where food is to be found.

In like manner Philip told Nathanael he had found the one sent by God, Jesus of Nazareth. When Nathanael scoffed at this, Philip's words were to the point: "Come and see!" he said. (John 1:46.) Later, when the woman at the well in Samaria discovered in Jesus a revelation of herself, she hurried to her kinsmen: "Come, see a man," she cried. (John 4:29.) Out of an experience of the reality of God's love for us, we share our gospel. "One thing I know, that though I was blind, now I see" (John 9:25) is an assurance that has started many of us on the path of witness, part of which inevitably for the Christian is the prayer of intercession, his priestly office.

A friend is sick or lonely or perplexed or wavering in spirit. In love for him and in love to God, we offer that friend through our intercession. Jesus did. Knowing the weakness of Simon Peter, Jesus said to him as they were leaving the upper room, "I have prayed for you that your faith may not fail." (Luke 22:32.) Paul went so far as to write "The Spirit helps us in our weakness; for we do not know how to pray as we ought, but the Spirit himself intercedes for us with sighs too deep for words." (Rom. 8:26.)

Our prayer should be a simple one, full of trust and love. It is not necessary to inform God in detail about the whole matter. "My friend is sick with migraine headaches. His business is not doing well, and his home life is quite disturbing, and his friends find him quarrelsome when really he's not that way when he's feeling all right." On and on we go, making sure that God has every last detail. Why do we do this? Because we have inside information that God does not possess? Because he has been too busy trying to solve an international problem to notice the minor problems of our friend? Do we really believe that we know more about it than God himself does?

How often we think it necessary to tell God just what to do. "Now that I have told you all about him, you'll see that this is what should be done about it. You should make him go to church—or heal him of his sickness—or give him this new job—or teach her to pick up her things—or make her behave as a young lady should." Or whatever it is that in our superior knowledge we see God should do in the situation. Are we that much smarter than God that we need to tell him just what to do? Is it perhaps that we want to make sure that our way, rather than his way, should be done?

Worse yet, how often we think it necessary to argue with God, trying to persuade him to do for our friend that we wish to have done! Does not the parable of the importunate widow, as well as the parable of the man with a midnight visitor (Luke 18:1-8; 11:5-8), suggest that we should pray on and on and on, until we get our desire? No, for neither one says we should try to persuade God to do what we want. Each one stresses a single point—that we should persevere in our prayer. We are not to pray one day, then skip a week or two, returning to it when we feel like it. We must be faithful, regular, persevering, if our prayer is to be meaningful. Prayer is not to persuade him to do what we desire.

Prayer is not to change God. It is to change us. To inform God about all the details, to tell him just what to do, to argue with him, is all wrong. To work hard with groanings and fastings as we pray, that God will be persuaded to do as we desire, is to manipulate him. We are not to use God. He is to use us. When we try to use him, to manipulate him, he becomes little more than a puppet on a stick to be worked for *my* desires. That is why there should be no demanding in intercessory prayer, no worrying God to do our will. He is God the Creator. We are man the creature.

Examine your intercession. Do you tell God every little detail about the one for whom you pray—even about her "Aunt Jenny, who is so aggressive that she never had a chance to think for herself"? As you search for a sympathetic background out of which can come your active help at the close of the prayer, do not waste time "informing" God all about it. Make your offering of the person for whom you are concerned, and then wait quietly for God's response. Learn to listen and do not talk to him so much.

When you pray for someone else, do you tell God just what you think he ought to do? Of course, you will tell him what you hope can happen. You want your friend to be well, to be happy, to enjoy the fullness of life. "O God, save him" is the cry of humanity. Are you sure you know just what that means? Are you willing to let God make his own decision about the manner of that saving?

Is your prayer simple, straight-forward, loving? Does it reveal complete trust in his mercy and his wisdom? Then make your intercession, leave it in God's love, and go about your business.

THE
TWENTY-FIRST WEEK

The Meditation

O THOU WHO ART MY FRIEND, THE SOURCE OF ALL COMRADESHIP, I OFFER
unto thee my loneliness. Thou, and thou alone, canst fill the void
within my days.

"All you need to do is to pray to God when you are lonely. You're
a Christian; you should know that!" I thank thee for my mean-well
friends, O God, but it is not as simple as that for me. I have prayed
unto thee. I do pray unto thee. Yet my loneliness remains. Humbly
I offer it to thee.

Sometimes it is because I am so young. Dreams fill my head, and
I live in the stars. How difficult it is to mark time with studies and
routine chores when the drums are calling me with stirring roll. I
believe it is thy purpose that I should listen to my own drummer,
but how lonely it is to march when others fail to hear the music or
to see the banners flying.

Thou knowest the bitter longings of my heart at the loss of a companion of the years. For a moment I have been glad to give my loved
one unto thee, but the ache remains, and the emptiness is renewed
every day. I open my mouth to speak—and no one is there. I
hurry in to help—and the room is bare. I hear a footstep on the
walk—but it belongs to another. O God, how long is the day,
and the night hours are past counting. Yet it has been thy strength
and thy comfort that has turned my darkness into morning.

Only thou understandest the heavy hearts of those like me who have grown old in years, who have watched friends and companions go before me. Alone I stand in a new and different generation, whose ways are not my ways, whose thoughts are not my thoughts. Confused at times, often afraid, I wonder what will become of me. Yet thou hast never left me, for thou art my refuge, and underneath are the everlasting arms of thy love.

In the deep searching of my heart to find thee, I have found thee face to face as thou hast found me. In joyous gratitude I have tried to tell others of the end—and the beginning—of my discovery, and I have been lost. I have no words to describe to the blind the Light that I have seen, nor to the deaf the Music that I have heard. Where are those whose eyes and ears are open to understand me? In loneliness I have turned away disappointedly, until through thy mercy I have been led to those who do understand. What joy then is mine, when I can share with another thy Light and thy Love!

Forgive me, O God, when I settle down in my loneliness, feeling sorry for myself. Grant me thy grace to accept my loneliness, to offer it unto thee in gratitude, for thou dost permit my loneliness to help me grow in spirit. Teach me to grow, O God, that I may help those who are lonelier than myself.

What Do You Really Want to Happen?

(INTERCESSION—4)

"Help me to pray for my sister," Millie asked. "She's in real trouble, but every time I'm with her lately we fight. She and her husband quarrel all the time, then they go out for the evening separately, both of them getting drunk. The next day she comes to me for help, but when I tell her to quit drinking and chasing around, to begin going to church again, just as we did when we were little girls, she gets angry with me. She says I'm always picking on her, that I don't love her. I'd do anything to help her. I pray for her every day but it doesn't do any good."

"What do you pray for her?"

"That God will stop her drinking and make her behave herself. He can't love her any more the way she is."

"You don't love her, do you? When you are with her, she says you are nagging her. And when you are not with her, then you nag at her through God, wanting him to pick on her. You don't really love her, do you? You're just exasperated with her."

She thought about this for a while. "Yes, that's so. I hadn't seen it that way. I don't love her, do I? If I did, I'd stop my nagging. I'm so upset about her carousing that I don't know what to do. I get so frustrated. I guess that is why I fly out at her every time I'm with her. Then I keep it up when I pray for her. That isn't love, is it?"

Millie must love her sister just as she is now—not as she might be, nor even as once she was. She cannot love the things she does, nor is that necessary, but she must love her sister regardless of her wrong actions.

More, she must believe that God too loves her sister, not in spite of, nor because of her actions, but in the midst of them, for such is his nature, and because he is love, he loves.

Millie is human. She cannot love like that, not at first. She can, however, begin with what love she has. It is the same for all of us.

Do you pray for a friend that he may know the love and joy and peace of God that you know? Or do you ask God to change his evil ways?

Do you lift him up in love before God? Or do you seek God's condemnation upon him?

First, begin with your true concern. What do you really want to happen? Do you want your husband—or your wife—to attend church? Or do you want him to know like you the wonder of God's grace and love? Did Millie want an end to her sister's drinking—or the beginning of her real happiness?

It is not enough to pray that your teen-ager should want to stay at home. Rather, ask yourself why he is bored at home. What is the attraction that draws him away from his parents? What are you doing to help him want to choose home first? Is it not your true concern that he should find a zest and joy in his coming manhood?

Once a woman joined a prayer class "so my husband will be home all the time." He had a responsible sales position with a large corporation and frequently was away a week or two at a time. At the end of the year he purchased a small store in a small city almost five hundred miles away, and now he is home every evening. "That isn't what I wanted!" she complained. "We've moved away from my church and my friends and everything I've loved!" Yet she has her husband home every evening.

So it is with an alcoholic, a cantankerous employee, a disagreeable neighbor, or anyone else for whom you are concerned. Find the basic root of that concern, what you really wish to have happen when you bring that friend to God.

Second, offer the person for whom you intercede just as he is. Do not apologize to God for him, nor affirm or deny his good or bad qualities. Say something like this: "Here is my sister, whose happiness I long for. You know just what she is and why she is like that. So I bring her in love to you, for you understand her, and you know my love for her. I place her in your keeping just as she is. I love her, and I would love her more. Help me to love her as you love her."

How can you "love" a cantankerous employee or a disagreeable neighbor? You can't—not at first. Tell God quite honestly that you do not like this person, and certainly you do not feel you can love him. Yet you know God does, so offer him to God's love. Seek God's blessing upon him each day, even when you cannot bless him. Be persistent in this daily prayer, and after a week or two you will note a change in your feeling toward that person. You cannot pray honestly day in and day out for a person, that God's blessing may rest upon him, without a change of heart within yourself.

Third, thank God for what he is doing in response to your intercession. You bring your friend in love, knowing that God will receive him in his love. Thank him for his love, for receiving your friend, for listening to your intercession. Then thank him for the work of his spirit in you, as well as in your friend. You may not know all that is happening, and none of it may be just what you had hoped for, but with trust in his love and faith in his wisdom—and a listening ear to his direction for you—arise and go in peace.

THE
TWENTY-SECOND WEEK

The Meditation

THOU HAST NEVER BEEN; THOU WILT NEVER BE; FOR THOU ART. PAST AND future have nothing to do with thee, for thou art ever present. In the finiteness of thy creature man, his span is bound by things past and things to come, but thou art the eternal one, the ever-present one, in whom there is neither yesterday nor tomorrow.

Forgive me, O God, when I live in the past. Old ways are familiar ways to me. "We have always done it that way" is my well-meant motto. It is easier for me, requiring less thought, less courage. Thou knowest the troubles that are mine even when all goes well. How can I be expected to face change with its unknown dangers? The past has taught me to heed the good old days. I have found in thee the assurance for my convictions, the certainty for my faith. Forgive me when I refuse the new just because it is new or hold to the old just because it is old.

Forgive me, O God, when I live in the morrow. My dreams are dreams of pleasantness and all my paths are peace. In the sweet by and by is my hope for fulfillment, the answer to all my weariness, my final escape from the vicissitudes of this life. Thou knowest, O God, how I wait for the morning when thou wilt bring me into the Promised Land. Then I will be up and doing, and life will be mine! Forgive me, O God, that in the meantime I huddle around a dying campfire, hoping for light, instead of seeking wood to put on the flame.

This is thy day. Now is thy time. O thou ever-present one, whose eternity is in this moment, teach me to live in the fullness of time with thine eternity in my heart. Give me this day bread for the day. Feed me, O God, with thy love that is pressed down, shaken together, running over.

Grant that I may take each day as it comes, grateful to thee for its fresh opportunities to know thee, to love thee, to serve thee. Accept, I pray thee, each moment of my day, that its sacrament may be a joy to thee, a blessing to me. Thou art the ever-present one, Spirit Eternal, God of Love.

For the Healing of the Spirit

(INTERCESSION—5)

Most prayers of intercession concern the health of the one prayed for. This is inevitable, since our health and the health of others close to us is probably more important to most of us than any other facet of our living. Read the newspaper and magazine advertisements and listen to radio and television commercials about drugs and medicines and aids to health to see how much these are part of the life of Americans. Even in less sophisticated areas of the world, physical survival is of major concern.

Only the foolish person substitutes prayer for the skills of medical science. Some religious sects, in all good conscience, refuse physical aids of any kind in the treatment of their ills. Most folk, however, willingly accept any help available for the protection and cure of their families—even prayer! Unfortunately, there are foolish people who turn to prayer only as a last resort, or those who are so foolish as to turn away completely from it.

Right prayer is a supplement to medical science. It undergirds the doctor and the nurse, including with the patient all who minister to his needs, physically, mentally, or spiritually. It is not "brought in" at the last minute, an emergency measure. It is a vital part of the daily life of a praying Christian. Yet in time of need the prayer of intercession, like the effectual, fervent prayer of any righteous man, avails much.

We have already noted that it is wrong to inform God all about an illness, or to tell him just what cure we have in mind—nor do we demand of him a certain action. Rather, in love we make an offering of the sick person to God, placing him consciously in God's love. He is, of course, in God's love already, as are all of us, but now we add our own love to God's love as we surround the patient with love.

Is it not best for those who pray for a person to know as much as possible about him? For some people this is a real help, since they find it difficult to pray for someone unknown to them. When a respected member of the community is seriously ill, large numbers of people, knowing him, pray for him. There is an emotional tie between them and their friend. Most people find it easier to pray for their own families than for a neighbor's. That is because most people, self-centered as we all are, are more interested in their own. The old prayer, though laughed at, is still true for many: "Lord, bless me and my wife, my son John and his wife, us four and no more."

One who has been learning the prayer that is love and the love that is prayer in these past few weeks does not need to know a thing about the person prayed for. Through my church or through my prayer class or through an acquaintance, I am asked to pray for a sick person whom I do not know. The one who asks me—minister, friend, neighbor —does know the person and is lovingly concerned for that person. I join my love, not to the love of the sick one whom I do not know, but to the love of the one I *do* know, and together we present our love to God, for he does not require of me knowledge at that time, only love. So Jesus in his recorded healings asks no questions about the person's family or social condition or even his medical history; in his love he healed the person when he could.

Physical healing, though, should be incidental to our prayer. What good is it for a man to be healed of a physical disease if he is embittered, despondent, world-sick, the rest of his days? Our prayer should be for wholeness of spirit, the total personality, peace of body and mind, the peace that does pass all understanding except for those who possess it. Whole and wholesome and holy and healthy all come from the same etymological root—the complete, the full circle, the "be ye perfect" of Jesus, the whole man physically and mentally and spiritually. We offer the total person to God in selfless love.

Consider these various ways of making your intercession. Leslie Weatherhead suggests that in imagination you should enter the sick room and stand at the foot of the bed. See, standing there at the side of the patient, Jesus the compassionate, whose loving hands are blessing the sick one. Join your love, he says, to the love of Jesus. Instead of the tired, worn face of the patient, see him whole again, fresh, alert, radiant.

If you do know the patient, so that you can bring his face to mind, regardless of the pattern of your intercession, always see him well, not sick. Do not send out to him any thoughts of pity, of incompleteness, of unwholesomeness. Let your prayer always be positive, dynamic, whole.

You may wish to make your intercession in connection with the observance of the Sacrament of Holy Communion. This may be in a public service, in which you will silently receive the elements in the name of the sick person, or your minister may arrange for you and a friend or two, or even for an entire prayer class, a private service, in which there will be prayers of intercession followed by the sacrament itself.

Often folk will hold a brief service of intercession, in which the laying on of hands will be part of the liturgy. Persons present will be proxies for the sick, kneeling before the altar and receiving the laying on of hands in the name of the sick. This follows the New Testament practice of Jas. 5:13-15, except that the sick person is not present. (If he were present, it would be a healing service, rather than a service of intercession.) Usually a minister administers the laying on of hands, but it is not at all necessary. A devout layman, ministering in the name of Christ, may equally well serve as God's agent.

Whether you are with a group or alone remember that it is neither the number of people nor the kind of service that is important. Be simple and direct in the offering of your intercession; make it brief but with your whole attention—God needs no haranguing—then conclude it with an act of thanksgiving.

THE
TWENTY-THIRD WEEK

The Meditation

MY GOD AND MY FATHER, SAVE ME FROM MY FRIENDS WHO THINK I AM going too far in my commitment to thee. I do not want to be called a fanatic, nor do I wish to be thought foolish. I do not mean to turn away from my friends—nor do I turn from them. Yet they believe that I am "too good" for them when I find it difficult to converse lightly as once I did.

Thou knowest I am not too good, nor do I feel in any way different from my friends. Thou hast drawn me to thyself with love, and I have found a way of life that opens new doors to my real self as well as to thee. I am full of gratitude to thee for all thou art doing to me, and I speak that gratitude openly. I do not intend to call attention to me, that thou knowest. I have done nothing, except to listen to thee, to respond to thy love. Thou art the one whom I would put to the fore.

O my Father, if I seek out only those whose searching speaks to mine, whose witness feeds my hungering spirit, forgive me. I need their fellowship, but I would not that its joy should cause pain of separation from those whom I have known and loved long. Nevertheless, thou art drawing me to those who love thee, who know thee. I am finding in them the companionship unknown in what once I thought were true friendships. When I visit with some former friends, I seem to be talking against walls of misunderstanding and suspicion.

Sometimes those closest to me think I am "strange" in my religion. I remember how the kinsfolk of Jesus, puzzled by the crowds around him, disturbed by the things he did after he left home, came to "take charge of him," thinking he was mad.[1] I would not do a thing to be thought queer, to be noticed among others, to be thought overly religious. Yet if the joy that thou hast given to me makes me "mad," I would rather be thy madman than live in the "sanity" I once knew.

O God, help me to live with others in loving regard, with sympathetic understanding. Forbid that consciously or unconsciously I should cause the least barrier to rise between me and another. Yet grant me the courage, O God, to hold to thee, to serve thee, to obey thee, regardless of the fears or misunderstandings of others. Thou art my life, and in thee would I live and move and have my being.

Taking Someone into the Light

(INTERCESSION—6)

In the fourteenth century Catherine of Siena was a woman of prayer and action. Through her efforts largely, the captivity of the papacy was ended. The papal seat was returned to Rome from Avignon after nearly seventy-five years. Catherine is best remembered, however, because of her life of prayer.

One day one of her serving maids came to her in great distress. "Dear mistress," she begged, "pray for my husband. The pain of his cancer is so intense that he is blaspheming God. Pray God that he will remove the pain and forgive my husband's blasphemy."

"No, I can't do that," Catherine replied. "God does not want him to have the pain, and God understands your husband's blasphemy. But when I go into the Light, I will take him into the Light with me."

The next day the maid came to Catherine again. "Thank you, dear

[1] See Mark 3:21 (Phillips, Knox); "out of his mind" (Moffatt, Goodspeed, Weymouth); "beside himself" (K.J.V., R.S.V.).

mistress, for your prayer for my husband. The pain has not lessened, but he seems to be able to stand it now. And he is no longer blaspheming God. Instead, he is praising God." Three days later the husband died, praise upon his lips.

For several weeks we have been learning the principles of intercessory prayer, and in our exercises we have been practicing the prayer that is love and the love that is prayer. We have seen that intercession may be of all sorts and kinds for individuals and causes, but that the foundation of all prayers of intercession is love for God and man. Without this our prayers are only empty phrases.

Now let us turn to a way of wordless intercession that many practice, the taking of someone into the Light. Suppose that your friend's name is Bill.

First, begin to concentrate. Close your eyes, eliminating all outside images. Then "see" Bill's face in the blackness. His image probably will be faint and will be competing with others to come. Slowly and carefully, without forcing, bring Bill's face into the center of that blackness. Do not be discouraged that other images come. Patiently bring back Bill's face until finally it is alone in the darkness of the closed eyes.

Sounds will distract you, but do not attempt to seal your ears. As you give closer and closer attention to Bill the sounds will lessen in volume until you will hardly hear any except unusual or loud ones. More, do not fight either with sounds or images as they come to the mind. Accept them, recognize them, then return to Bill's image.

As the attention becomes sharper so that Bill's features are distinct, see him with smiling, happy face. Never be negative, holding a tired, sad, dull face in your mind's eyes. It is the positive, awakened, radiant Bill that you want to offer to God.

Breathe regularly and slowly. As you focus your attention even more sharply, almost hold your breath. Then pinpoint Bill's face, so that every other image is gone. At that moment Bill's face will appear centered in what seems to be a circle of light.

For most people this centering will last for only a second. In time it will increase as one's practice of concentration continues, perhaps for several seconds, perhaps even for a full minute. In the instant of the centering of the face in the light, make your offering of love, perhaps with a brief "God bless Bill." Then later when you become more proficient use only a single phrase, such as "O God," at the very instant of awareness that Bill is now in the light. It will not be so much a part of your intercession as a sudden awareness of the presence of God, an ejaculation of adoration, of humility.

Do this same thing with the faces of others for whom you would pray, until you find that within a minute or two you can bring into focus a face. The intensity of the moment, with its full and total attention, is a sufficient offering of love. If the mind wavers for a bit, however, or other images come before you have completed your focusing, begin over again.

Sometimes the urging of the Spirit may compel you to hold a person a second and a third time, and if the sense of compulsion is there accept it. It is his spirit working within you. Then release it, and move on to the next person on your list.

Second, concentration now being quite simple for you—this may take weeks and not days, but persevere in it, realizing that some find it easier than others—begin to eliminate the image of Bill's face. Become still and bring the *thought* of Bill into the circle of light. Say the name inwardly as the focused light appears, holding it as long as you can in loving offering, then let it go, moving on to the thought of the next person.

It is in this stage of your growing that you will find it easy to pray for those whom you do not know. You no longer need an image for your intercession. You can offer John's friend or Mary's sister, even though you have not known or seen them.

In this total attention there is the beginning of deep awareness of the presence of God. You will then discover two facts. First, intercession no longer is hard, long, tedious work, in which words stumble over themselves. Instead, it is a simple offering of love, the intensity of the full attention for a moment being far superior to worded prayers intermingled with many distracting images over a length of time. These wordless prayers may be lifted up dozens of times during the day, wherever one may happen to be.

Second, and far more significant for our growing in the life of prayer, you will find that this total attention is indeed the avenue to contemplative prayer. You will find that as you bring the thought of a person into the Light that is the presence of God, you will forget yourself and the one for whom you pray. Instead, you will rest in his light.

Do not, then, hasten to return to the next person on your list. Stay with that Presence as long as you can. When you become aware of yourself once again and the wonder of your experience finds expression in thanksgiving or adoration, then move on to the next on your list. At the close of your intercession, go on about your work, taking with you the sense of his presence. This is the beginning of the prayer without ceasing, a life like that of Brother Lawrence which, though in the midst of business or recreation, in the kitchen or office or chapel, is practicing the presence of God.

THE
TWENTY-FOURTH WEEK

The Meditation

How do i love thee, o god? i love thee with all my heart and with all my soul and with all my mind and with all my strength.

I love Thee, O thou one God, with my whole self, the real self, the self that asks for nothing, seeks for nothing, the self which is That of God within me; with the wholeness of my personality, that which makes me an individual, different from all other persons, unique in thine eyes, even though counted like all others in the eyes of the world; with the very essence of my being, that which is the true "I," do I love thee.

I love thee, O thou Creator of all life, as thy creature; made out of the dust in thine own image; molded by thy hands; inspired by thy breath; placed upon thy earth where I may know birth and death, the full life cycle with its pain and sorrow, its pleasure and joy. Through thy compassion thou didst give me a helpmeet that I should not endure alone the days of my years, and in and through that companionship do I love thee.

I love thee, O thou Eternal Spirit, as one whose soul's invincible surmise is grounded in the indomitable hope thou hast fixed in my breast that I am a living soul. Thou art, and I am, and this is life eternal, that I may know thee, the only true God, and Jesus Christ whom thou hast sent.

I love thee, O my Father, for thou hast first loved me. Thou, the Eternal One, before whose awe and majesty I bow in reverent worship, before whose holiness I kneel with covered head, thou, the Father of my Lord Jesus Christ, and my Father, dost draw me to thyself with cords of love. With longing dost thou long for me, as one who stands at the door and knocks, as a Father peering into the distance from his housetop, as the Hound of Heaven whose strong feet follow, follow after.

How do I love thee, O God? I love thee with all my heart and with all my soul and with all my mind and with all my strength.

The Heights of Prayer

(ADORATION—1)

Now we come to the one prayer that has nothing whatever of self-interest, not even a hint of "using" God. It is the prayer of adoration, the awareness of the glory of God.

> Bless the Lord, O my soul;
> and all that is within me, bless his holy name!
> Bless the Lord, O my soul. (Ps. 103:1-2.)

It does not go on to say "and forget not all his benefits." That is the prayer of thanksgiving. It is a necessary prayer, a most significant one.

This goes beyond thanksgiving. It is adoration, praise to God for what he is, not for what he does. It is the cry of Isaiah:

> Holy, holy, holy is the Lord of hosts;
> the whole earth is full of his glory. (Isa. 6:3.)

It is the doxology that concludes the Lord's Prayer: "For thine is the kingdom, and the power, and the glory."

John Casteel, in his excellent study *Rediscovering Prayer,* suggested that adoration is the real beginning of true prayer. "Although . . . prayer includes modes of communion, such as confession, thanksgiving, and intercession, the life of prayer in its fullness has been found by those who have persevered in it to begin in the adoration of God, as well as to end there." [1] Yet Dr. Casteel recognized the difficulty here, for he realized that for many spiritual teachers adoration is a high form of prayer not to be considered on the low level of other prayer. Evelyn Underhill, for one, placed adoration at the end of prayer, its culmination, as I am doing in this series of exercises. For me it is the height of prayer, the peak to which we must aspire. Only out of a full life of prayer can come the completely unselfish prayer of adoration.

Nevertheless, adoration does have its beginning. As I have written about the prayer of thanksgiving, so the first acts of adoration must be consciously uttered words and phrases repeated over and over again. Then that beginning will lead to its true ending, as Casteel wrote: "So the adoration of God becomes for us both the beginning and the goal of the life of prayer: the first act undertaken with whatever love and power we now command, and the last act left us after a long life offered in the praise and service of his glory." [2]

Begin your exercise, then, with conscious acts of adoration. Begin simply by saying: "I adore thee, O God. Sing praises, O my heart, unto your God. Blessed be thy holy name." These are most simple acts, largely only words in the beginning, but their constant repetition becomes the habitual act through which the emotional attitude of praise and adoration grows.

Choose a phrase that seems to be your *attrait.* Repeat it over and over again until its words sing in your mind and heart.

"Bless the Lord, O my soul."

"Glory be to Thee, O Lord."

---

[1] New York: Association Press, 1955, p. 23.
[2] *Ibid.,* pp. 23-24.

"Blessed be Thy name."

"My Lord and my God" (the phrase of the disciple Thomas).

"My God and my All" (the prayer of Francis of Assisi throughout one night).

In *The Way of a Pilgrim* [3] the anonymous author told of his search for the prayer without ceasing. Throughout his native Russia a century ago, he questioned preachers, abbots, laymen, but none gave him the way. Then a lonely staret, a poor monk, teaches him to say repeatedly the prayer of Jesus: "Lord Jesus Christ, have mercy on me."

Although few will wish to repeat their prayer the thousands of times that the Pilgrim did, if you would really move from mere words to living phrases, so that your heart truly is lifted into adoration, say over and over again your chosen phrase. While lying awake at night, upon rising, during frequent pauses in the day, in the quiet before you go to sleep, offer your prayer of adoration to God.

[3] Translated from the Russian by Reginald M. French (New York: Harper & Brothers, undated).

THE
TWENTY-FIFTH WEEK

The Meditation

THANKS BE UNTO THEE, O PENETRATING LIGHT, THAT THOU ART SHOWING TO me the disease of self-love. Into the hidden corners of my heart thy rays of holiness are shining their truth, revealing with judgment and with love my pride.

Just when I think that I have finally pulled out the last roots of pride so that I can sit back in my ease and rejoice in my achievement, thou dost show me tiny rootlets still alive. I am impatient that I have not grown as fast as I believe I should by this time. Am I not a most sensitive person to things spiritual? Then should I not be making more progress?

I am disappointed when I have little power to check continual irritations that arise over unimportant matters. Surely anyone with my intelligence should have better self-control than that! I am chagrined that others seem to have more of God's love than I do. I know I have served him to the best of my ability.

I am surprised that one with my knowledge should have so meager an understanding of himself. Have I not looked within ere this time? Have I never probed beneath the surface up to now? How much of me is yet hidden to my consciousness, submerged like the great mass of an iceberg?

In thy mercy, O God, keep the rays of thy holiness pointed directly into my heart, until every bit of me is uncovered, every unknown fault made known, every hidden posture laid bare. Teach me to accept that thou dost reveal, to confess my weakness, to reach for thy forgiveness.

Grant, O merciful God, that I may have courage to face the truth thou dost disclose, insight to act rightly upon my discovery, and humility to know that only through thy constant help is there any cure for this disease of self-love.

Loving God "for Nothing"

(ADORATION—2)

Highest of all loves is that which asks nothing, seeks nothing, gives nothing, not even itself, which is one's greatest sacrifice. Rare is the man who loves like that; yet at times, in the prayer of adoration, each one of us for a moment may love with that degree of selflessness.

Man wants a return for his loving, if it is nothing more than approval or acceptance. He can love without asking or seeking, but in his giving he is disappointed if he is not accepted. God alone can love in fullness without any thought of return to himself. Bernard of Clairvaux suggested that there are four levels of love: The love of the self, the love of God for the self, the love of God and the self for the sake of God, and finally, the love of God with no thought whatever of the self. Being a realist, he added, "I do not know if the fourth is reached in its perfection by any man in this life."

God only loves with no thought of himself. Even in the giving of himself through Christ Jesus he did not want anything for himself. It is the nature of God as love to love without hint or suggestion of reward for that loving. God does not think of success or failure, of pleasure or pain, of joy or sorrow, of acceptance or rejection.

Man does—yet not all men. The old tale of the woman of Alexandria suggests that she thought some could go beyond self, loving God without attachment. She went through the streets one day carrying a pitcher of water in one hand, a burning torch in the other. "What is the meaning of the two objects?" she was asked. "I am going to burn the ramparts of heaven and quench the fires of hell," she answered. "Then men will love God without thought of reward to be gained or punishment to be avoided."

Edward Caswall's translation of the hymn attributed to Francis Xavier also hints that man can love at times with the detached love of God:

> My God, I love thee; not because
> I hope for heaven thereby,
> Nor yet because who love thee not
> Are lost eternally;
>
> Not with the hope of gaining aught;
> Not seeking a reward;
> But as thyself hast loved me,
> O ever-loving Lord,
>
> E'en so I love thee, and will love,
> And in thy praise will sing,
> Solely because thou art my God,
> And my eternal King.

Hubert sought and found help from a minister not his own pastor. In puzzled gratitude he said to his counselor one day, "Why are you helping me, when I do not attend your church? You are good for nothing, aren't you?" God is like that, "good for nothing," loving without demanding return. We too can love God "for nothing," as we offer him our praise and adoration.

In *The Troubled Border* T. D. Allen wrote of the Indian wife of a trader for the Hudson's Bay Company, who was compelled by her inner spirit to leave her tent one night.

Marguerite . . . stood, drinking in her fill of the night and then strolled on entranced. Coming to a table rock extending over the waters, she stepped out and, instinctively, lifted her arms, spreading them wide and upward. "Merci" she whispered.

It was just something she did, not exactly a prayer. Prayers, she said on her knees. Also a prayer asked for more and, at these moments, Marguerite would never think of asking for more. And yet the Great Spirit was in this rite of hers. He heard her, she knew. He was out there listening, and he knew that within her outspread arms she was including, as of a piece with all this beauty, her children and her Johnny. He knew that she was saying thank you and feeling a little guilty because she possessed more than her share of love and goodness.

And the way she knew he was there was that, whenever she stopped like this, night or day, just to be glad for things as they were and to murmur, "Merci," the Great Spirit answered.

"Merci," he whispered back and when she heard it the moon grew brighter for an instant and made her warm.[1]

Last week we practiced the use of repetitive phrases as a discipline consciously to create in us such an awareness of God's glory. Now let us take a single word, lifting it repeatedly with affection to God. The anonymous author of *The Cloud of Unknowing* said it should be a word of one syllable, like "love," "God," or any other such word whose one syllable will sing within us. Do not think about it, he suggested, but repeat your chosen word over and over again, a discipline for the will.

For myself I have fallen into the phrase "O Father," with which my heart's longing finds expression in joy, in sorrow, in faith, in doubt, in light, in darkness. It was not a conscious choice, but came naturally after months of practicing a single word. I had said over and over again "love" or "peace" or "joy" or "God" as conscious efforts to love God for himself, as himself, with no thought of return to me or to another, when suddenly I realized that for some time I had been using

[1] New York: Harper & Brothers, 1954, pp. 53-54.

the phrase "O Father." It has now become my own, without conscious effort on my part.

Take a single word, or if it seems wise, a two-syllable word, like "Jesus" or "Father," and repeat it many times day in and day out. When in the course of time the repetition is no longer intellectual but emotional, not the action of the mind but of the will, it will become your own, the song of your heart, sung in adoration.

THE
TWENTY-SIXTH WEEK

The Meditation

O GOD, MY GOD, HOW THOU HAST LAID THY HANDS UPON ME! I TREMBLE before thee, the Holy One of Israel.

Before I was born thou didst choose for me my parents and their parents. From them and through them thou didst bring a rich heritage to me. The shape of my body, the color of my eyes, the size of my fingers, the texture of my hair all come from them. My disposition, the quality of my mind, the predominant emotions that mark my temperament, are thy gifts to me through them.

Through the years of my childhood and youth thou hast placed me in a family, in a home, in the midst of a community, where love and fellowship have nurtured my spirit. A host of passers-by, touching momentarily my mind and heart, have brought healing to my spirit as the shadow of Peter along the by-ways of Jerusalem fell with blessing upon the sick laid in his path. Many of these I can no longer name, and others are but dim memories from a distant past, but thou didst quicken my life as they touched me.

Events have piled upon events in the days of my years. Sometimes I have been bitter, and sometimes I have been patient. But all the time thou hast been my God, my Father, in whose hands I have been lifted up. Time and again I have fallen in despair, and always thou didst in love wait for me to turn to thy care and providence, that I might be raised upon my feet.

O God, my God, great and wonderful are thy ways in this day of my life. Still art thou my God. Still dost thou hold me in the hollow of thy hands. Still art thou the one to whom alone I can come in all my foolishness and all my sin, and know that thou dost love me, that thou dost forgive me, that thou dost bless me. O Lord most holy, Lord most high, here am I, take me.

New Lives for Old

(ADORATION—3)

In the continual lifting up of the heart in awe and wonder and love before and to the one who indeed is Reality, our prayer of adoration becomes that intense awareness, "lost in wonder, love, and praise," which is existential knowledge. The presence of God, the *numinous* that reveals the *mysterium tremendum* of Rudolph Otto's memorable phrase, is known intuitively with a certainty as great as or even greater than sensual awareness of a physical relationship. What has been known *about* God through reason is now one's actual experience *of* God through intuition.

This state of awareness is normally quite brief. Such is its intensity that an entire lifetime seems to be compressed into a few moments. In another figure, the whole universe—the earth, the seas, the sky, the distant spaces of vast and unknown worlds—seems to be held in the hollow of one's hands or in the embrace of one's arms. Here is the true meaning of ecstasy, not some weird and fanciful vision of floating on the clouds or even of dwelling in an imaginary paradise, but "being beside oneself," that psychological state of total absorption in Reality whose concentration is accompanied by almost complete loss of sense perception for a time. In simple analogy it is much like the common absorption in daydream or intense thought that causes a friend to say, "Hi there! Wake up! Where have you been the past few minutes? You seemed beside yourself!" Of course you were "beside yourself," in a state of true ecstasy, because of your awareness of the presence of God, define it how you will.

This experience may take on most unusual forms for a few people. Raynor C. Johnson in *Watcher on the Hills*,[1] a study of mysticism in the lives of "ordinary" persons, described some quite unusual extra-sensory perceptions in which the awareness of Reality leads into strange visions. He also writes about the use of hypnosis and drugs in inducing states of awareness similar to that of certain mystics. These latter particularly are for the rare or unusual individual and are not at all to be sought out by the most of us as a part of our life of prayer. Only under the control of trained researchers should any such experiments be entered into. Yet the experiences described by Johnson are frequent enough that we should know about them.

Much more common are moments of "revelation," when one *knows* that God has spoken to him. Among the classic examples of revelation are that of Isaiah in the temple, Saul on the road to Damascus, Juliana of Norwich in her sickbed, George Fox in the open fields of England, John Wesley in his room at Aldersgate. Each of these, and an untold number of others, had a revelation of God's presence so profound that their lives were completely changed.

As far as we know, Isaiah and Juliana of Norwich never again had such visions of the Reality That Is. The one became a prophet and statesman for forty years, never forgetting the holiness and faithfulness of the Lord whom he had seen in the year that King Uzziah died. (See Isa. 6.) The other continued to be a recluse in her native Norwich for more than forty years after her "shewings" on Sunday morning, May 8, 1373. She sought anonymity for herself, and the little we know is in her *Revelations of Divine Love,* with its eighty-six chapters of her attempt through the years to interpret for others the God who revealed himself to her in her youth.[2]

---

[1] New York: Harper & Brothers, 1959.

[2] Cf. P. Franklin Chambers, ed., *Juliana of Norwich* (New York: Harper & Brothers, 1955).

Saul of Tarsus; George Fox, the Quaker; John Wesley, founder of Methodism; all had repeated revelations of the presence of God, though none with the intensity of their first "seeing" of the Lord. All five of theses persons, and this is equally true of many lesser known individuals, whether they had one all-encompassing vision or a series of revelations diminishing in power and intensity, continued their practice of adoration throughout their lives. Hence, though their states of intense awareness were very brief, their daily awareness of God and his world was considerably heightened.

This is true even today for those who would in nowise call themselves masters in the life of prayer. Yet we have known a real awareness of his presence in the total impact of sight and sound and taste and smell and touch, the sensual world accepted with joy, part of our total response to the fullness of nature and of nature's God. That awareness is an abandonment to the moment, a full concentration of the entire self upon an event, being washed by it, submerged in it.

One's spiritual horizons are expanded by this limitless physical awareness, a breadth of excitement completed only by the full circle of 360 degress. It is true living, completely outside of oneself, wholly within oneself. It is a synthesis that gathers together isolated facts into truth. I like to picture this in the form of a child captured by wonder: "Eyes bright, ears alert, lips slightly parted, the nostrils twitching, the flesh taut, the fingers spread, the head lifted—the attention of the whole being." For me this is the heart of contemplation, dwelling in the inmost sanctuary, in the very mind of God.[3]

The five men and women of the interior life mentioned above, and hosts of others, are quite like us today in this respect: Out of their awareness of the glory of God and his holiness and their constant practice of the prayers of adoration came new lives for old. They differ from us only in the degree of their first vision, of their continuing com-

[3] Cf. Ch. on "Awareness" in Harold Wiley Freer, *Christian Disciplines* (New York: Pageant Press, Inc., 1960).

mitment, and of their natural endowments. In the light of whatever vision we have, in accordance with the totality of our commitment, and subject to the natural talents which God has given us, our lives are equally changed through the grace of God.

How has God changed your life through your own humble awareness of his glory?

THE
TWENTY-SEVENTH WEEK

The Meditation

BLESSED BE THY NAME, O GOD. WITH WONDER I LOOK INTO THY FACE.

I see thee in the simple trust of a little child. How he does reach out his hand to me with almost casual abandonment, as he puts his life into mine. Without question, without qualification, but in complete assurance, he accepts me in his love. I am his, and he is mine—and thou art glad too, O God.

I see thee in the questing of youth, their desire for freedom, their search for truth, their hunger for recognition. Thou dost cause them to stand up on their own feet, even at the risk of open rebellion, even at the price of loneliness. Thou hast given them verve, enthusiasm, a tireless energy that sometimes spins the heads of older folk by its dizzy pace. Thou art in their painful growing, and thou dost delight in their unfolding.

I see thee in the purposiveness of the middle years. By strength of mind and spirit, through years of hard work, backed by persistent effort to know and to understand the meaning with which thou hast undergirded their lives, they come into the fullness of adulthood. Families, work, friendship, they have achieved—and they have not been content, for thou hast led them to search for thy purpose in their lives to make meaningful their days. Fretful searching becomes quiet seeking, lives offered to thee in open commitment. Thou dost bless and accept that commitment, O God, placing thy mark upon their spirits.

I see thee in the ripening years, when the pace of the body slows down and the wisdom of past experience bears fruit in outgoing mind and warm heart and gentle spirit. In the maturity of these quiet days thou hast dispelled the need for status, the ambition to achieve, the demand for recognition. Thy saints of mellowed days *know*. Thou art their God, the source of their love, of their patience, of their assurance. They wait for thee as the ripening grain waits for the harvest.

Blessed be thy name, O God, for thou dost reveal thy face to me in many ways.

Merging the Spiritual Life with the Material

(LOVE IN ACTION—4)

Prayers of adoration lead almost inevitably into the heart of contemplation, in which we stand in awe before God, ourselves forgotten for a moment. Such times come with increasing number as we progress in the life of prayer, yet they are always new, always startling moments, continually surprising us with their joy. It is a serious temptation for us to seek permanently these experiences, even if it means our living apart from the world, for here seems to be "spiritual" living.

Meister Eckhart in the fourteenth century warned against this kind of travesty against Christian faith when he wrote:

Those who are given to the life of contemplation and avoid activities deceive themselves and are on the wrong track. I say that the contemplative person should indeed avoid even the thought of deeds to be done during the period of his contemplation but afterwards he should get busy, for no one can or should engage in contemplation all the time, for active life is to be a respite from contemplation.[1]

So he emphasized, "If a person were in such a rapturous state as St.

---

[1] Raymond B. Blakney, *Meister Eckhart* (New York: Harper & Brothers, 1941), p. 238. Used by permission.

Paul once entered, and he knew of a sick man who wanted a cup of soup, it would be far better to withdraw from the rapture for love's sake and serve him who is in need." [2]

That is love in action. Our contemplation gives us the deep source out of which our service to God and man may be fulfilled.

Consider how many of the contemplatives of the past and the present were men and women of action, recognizing the danger of limiting themselves to one aspect of the Mary-Martha life. The Desert Fathers, for example, withdrew from the cities and towns into the wilderness near the breakdown of the Roman Empire. Founding monasteries, they sought to deepen their search for personal knowledge of the reality of God in quiet living. These centers of contemplation became hospitals, schools, dormitories for thousands of refugees fleeing from war and poverty. The monks themselves worked hard in their own fields, and many hired out at harvest, that they might have extra grain for the poor in prisons and relief stations along the Mediterranean shore. Because of their combination of contemplation and action the Church survived.

Benedict and Bernard of Clairvaux both required that prayers of contemplation should be fulfilled with work for others. Francis of Assisi gave long hours to the sick. Catherine of Siena, whose life was largely prayer, was the realistic politician through whose efforts the Great Schism was ended, restoring the papacy to Rome. Her namesake, Catherine of Genoa, longed to remain before the altar in prayer, yet for more than a quarter-century she administered most efficiently a large hospital.

Vincent de Paul insisted upon strict observances of interior prayer, yet his vast system of charities spread throughout France. Teresa of Avila, probably the best known of all contemplatives, directed her own and other religious houses in Spain with a skill equal to that of many modern business executives.

[2] *Ibid.,* p. 14.

In more recent times Mahatma Gandhi, devout Hindu whose love in action more than anything else brought independence to India; Toyohiko Kagawa, Japanese Christian whose prayers were matched with indefatigable labor for lepers and the slum-poor; and Dorothy Day, founder of "The Catholic Worker" in New York and noted retreat leader and pacifist, all proved their love for God by their love for man.

What about yourself? Do you seek to become a truly "spiritual" person? Would you limit that phrase to separating yourself from the life of the world? Only a few rare souls are led by God into the vocation of contemplation itself. The most of us are placed in the midst of a world concerned with the material needs of food and lodging and care of the body and the mind.

What will you do in your own life to join together these two concerns—the needs of the spiritual world and the material world?

Perhaps you will enter politics—as a ward helper to stuff envelopes, to answer the telephone, to serve as general handyman; as a committeeman; or as a candidate for public office. Certainly you will cast your vote faithfully and encourage others to do the same.

Is there a place for you in your local unit of the National Conference of Jews and Christians, through which you may help prevent discriminatory action because of creed? Will you share in racial brotherhood projects, going beyond annual pulpit exchanges to seek dignity and honor for men of all races in meeting their needs for housing, for education, for employment?

Will you encourage young people to enroll in work camps here and abroad, volunteers willing to work hard physically and mentally as they share with other youth of different color, creed, or nationality? Could you arrange for an exchange of high-school pupils between your community and a foreign country, helping both with necessary finances and with adequate preparation within your own community for the acceptance of the foreign student?

Is there someone who will seek employment for released convicts, providing the means for rehabilitation for an entire family as one person is restored to usefulness? Is there someone to help with unwed mothers through a Crittenden Home or the like?

Listing opportunities for creative love in action would take many pages. The imaginative person, knowing himself and his talents, seeking through his minister or through a social agency means to implement his life of prayer, will not be at a loss. No work is too slight, too unimportant. It may bring no fame, no public reward, no monetary gain. If it is for any of those purposes, it is of the Devil, and not of God! If, however, it is work shared with a brother, in which the needs of both are met in Christian brotherhood, then it is love in action.

THE
TWENTY-EIGHTH WEEK

The Meditation

HOLY, HOLY, HOLY IS THE LORD OF HOSTS. THE WHOLE EARTH IS FULL OF
thy glory. The heavens above and the seas beneath speak of thee.
Thou art God, the Eternal One, the Ancient of Days.

O thou Eternal One, here is my prayer. I do not want anything; I
do not seek anything; I do not ask anything. Neither for myself nor
for another do I come unto thee.

Because thou art God, I bless thee. Because thou art love, I adore
thee. Because thou art thyself, I offer my prayer unto thee. Blessed
be thy holy name.

Upon the altar of my heart I would present myself unto thee, O God,
a living sacrifice, holy and acceptable unto thee. Like incense rising to
the heavens, so my prayers are lifted to thee, a gift for thyself with no
strings attached. Do with me as thou wilt, using me or not using me,
accepting me or not accepting me, blessing me or not blessing me. I
am thine, O Lord, wholly thine.

Sing, O my heart, sing unto the Lord. Sing praises unto him. O my
Father, I would bless thee. O my Father, I would love thee. O my
Father, I would serve thee. Thou art my life, my light, my love. In
thee, and in thee alone, is my joy.

Saying Yes to the Light

(COMMITMENT—1)

Last of the three prayers that show our love to God is the prayer of commitment, an awareness of our need for fulfillment through self-offering. It is pre-eminently a prayer of action. It is Isaiah's response to God's call: "Here I am! Send me." It is Luther's declaration of obedience: "Here stand I—I can do no otherwise. God help me. Amen." It is the total offering of self.

No matter how or what the encounter may be, when God meets us we do respond. Our action may be "yes" or "no." The choice is always ours, but a decision must be made. The prayer of commitment is saying yes to the light of that encounter.

Paul writes in Romans 12 that we are to present our bodies as a living sacrifice, holy and acceptable to God. So our commitment is to be a living sacrifice, a living offering to God. Let us not be fooled by adolescent zeal—regardless of age—that seeks romantic martyrdom, believing that it is significant to die for something. It is too easy to die for something, to glory in a kind of martyrdom in which *I* show what *I* can do. That is the glorification of the self, a sign of immaturity. Someone has said that the mark of the immature man is that he wants to die nobly for a cause, but that the mark of the mature man is that he wants to live humbly for one. It is not so easy to live for something, where there is no personal glory, only stubborn, humdrum, patient living, loving, giving, and serving. That is the commitment that God seeks, a living sacrifice.

This living sacrifice is a life made holy, and our holiness comes from obedience to God. It is his gift to us, when we change from serving self to serving him. He calls us, and then he grants us the power to turn from darkness to the light. Our allegiance to him must be complete, however, the sole kind of holiness that will be acceptable to God. It is an allegiance that is to be renewed daily, continuing dependence upon God throughout our life. This commitment, therefore, never comes to final fruition in this life; our deepening knowledge of God only leads us into an increasing awareness of our need for fulfillment through an ever-new, ever-expanding offering of the self.

Commitment belongs to all phases of our life, not just the religious aspect. Life is decision. When we refuse to choose, refuse to act, we die. In our eating we choose certan foods and beverages. We cannot wait to decide whether or not we like them, or they like us. We cannot wait until the final word is issued as to calories and vitamins. We choose to eat if we are to live, and later we learn to choose more carefully as our knowledge increases. We begin, however, by committing ourselves to action. We eat and drink—not just on the days that we feel like it, or in the months that have an "R" in them. We eat every day and every month—or we die.

Consider how we commit ourselves in marriage. It is whole or none. No wife wants a half-committed man—sharing him on week ends with another woman. Nor does the sensible man "experiment" with a wife for a year or two, a trial marriage. Two people give of themselves for life, each committing himself to the other, or the marriage is blasphemy against the sacredness of human life.

So it is with a job. Unless we give ourselves completely to it, that job becomes a burden, a joyless way to "make a living." No employer will keep long a worker who merely "plays" at it. Yet zest can be found in the most humble work when both the will and heart are in it.

In my seminary days two professors taught in the same department. Both were most conscientious men, scholars who continually spent hours in research. One published only two books in his lifetime, for he said his mind was always changing from day to day. The other published many books, yet his mind was growing too. He committed himself, though, to one point of view long enough to present it in writing, knowing that growth would require emendation in days to come, but for that one day, he gave himself completely to the idea as he knew it.

When we commit ourselves to God we cannot know him in his fullness. If we waited until we knew him completely we could never commit ourselves. We cannot wait until we know him. It is impossible to comprehend God, but it is possible to apprehend him. We give ourselves to the little we do know about him, put our trust in our beginnings, believing that as he gives himself more fully to us, he will then increase our trust.

It is so with love. The only way to know love is to give ourselves to love. Reading about it, discussing it with others, analyzing it in fiction and biography, is quite academic as compared with saying yes to the light of love. One knows a little about love; the other loves. The two are a world apart. Love, like God, is too vast for us to comprehend. It is simple enough for us to apprehend.

Begin your prayer of commitment, then, with the simple prayer of Isaiah: "Here I am! Send me." In this place where God at this moment has placed me I begin to obey him. I will not wait for a better place, a larger place, one that is in greater need of what I have. If in time he calls we elsewhere, that will be fine, but just now, I am here, and here is where God wants me to serve him.

How may I serve him where now I am—In my home, my work, my church, and my community?

More, it is I who am here, asking to be sent. I wish I were one with greater talents, with finer personality. But it is I, with what I have, small or large, who is offering myself in commitment. In Marc Connelly's *The Green Pastures* the Lawd told Noah to build an ark to save his family. Noah questioned this at first, wondering what qualifications he had that he should serve the Lawd. But Noah was finally smart enough to say of himself: "I ain' very much, but I'se all I got."

What do I have that I can give to him? Am I willing to give every bit of myself in obedience to God? or do I withhold a corner of myself?

Finally, I am offering myself: "Send me"—not another. How many times have I refused a task by saying, "There is Joe. He'll do a better job." Or "Why not ask Joan? She isn't doing as much as I am." I am like Peter, when Jesus told him to feed his sheep. Peter turned, and saw John standing a short distance away. "How about that man?" Peter wanted to know. "Never you mind what I have planned for him," Jesus answered. "You follow me!"

Am I willing to follow? To love? To comfort? To encourage? To help? To share? To strengthen?

Do I really mean it when I pray, "Here I am! Send me?"

THE
TWENTY-NINTH WEEK

The Meditation

O GOD, THOU KNOWEST THAT I WOULD SERVE THEE. THOU KNOWEST THAT
all that I am and all that I have I offer to thee. Would God that I
had more, but thou desirest what I have.

Accept me, O God, where I am. How wonderful it would be if I
might serve in some area of vast need, to be like the saints of old who
gave themselves without stint day and night. How they did work
among the poor, among orphans, with the sick, with the lepers, walking
the roads of the countryside in humble devotion, and plodding the city
streets on errands of mercy! O to give myself like that, in strange and
out-of-the-way places, where I might be thy servant!

Am I trying to choose the spot, my self-will to the fore, discontented
with the place in which thou hast put me? Is it the glamor of the
unusual, the romance of the different, that attracts me? Am I bored
with the routine of love in action in my own home, within the bounds
of my own community where the folk all know me for what I am?
Dost thou call me to serve where I am known, among people who long
have known my many weaknesses and my little strength? Is it here
where I now live that in truth thou wouldst have me serve?

Accept me, O God, with what I have. If only the Holy Spirit might
descend upon me that I might be a healer of body and mind. If only
the gift of evangelistic fervor could be mine that I might win multi-
tudes to thee. If only my heart did burn within that thy love in me

might ease the heartache of all who came to me. How I would serve thee if thou wouldst give me the desires of my heart.

Would I be serving thee—or me? Do I seek additional gifts from thee that I may be what I want to be, what I dream to be? Is it for myself that I seek more? Am I interested in what I might be able to do if only thou wouldst give me these new talents? Or am I interested in what Thou canst do, even with what I now have?

O God, thou knowest my inner heart. Thou knowest how strong is my longing to be used by thee in my way, in the places of my choice, through the abilities of my desire. Forgive me, O God, when I put myself first and thyself second, my desires and longings first and thine second. I believe I would give myself, all of me, just where I am, with what I have, to thee. I do believe; help thou my unbelief.

Clues to the Meaning of Surrender

(COMMITMENT—2)

In all prayers words are important, but of far greater importance is the inner attitude. Especially is this true with the prayer of commitment, which is essentially a prayer of action. It is not enough to pray, "Here I am! Send me." One must rise up and go. Otherwise, the prayer is meaningless, a fraud, no better than Augustine's "Grant me chastity and continence, but not yet."

Basic to all other action in the prayer of commitment is the surrender of the self to God. Whether we come or go or stand, whether we say yes or no or maybe, whether we ask or seek or knock or find, these actions are but implementations of the supreme action: Surrender. It is the total offering of the self to him out of which will come all lesser actions.

As clues to the meaning of surrender, let us consider three biblical passages. The first of these tells of the last days of Joshua, when the old leader was about to die. He called his tribes together, still a loosely knit people, admonishing them to choose the Lord in preference to the gods from across the river. Whether or not the people did choose the Lord, he declared, "As for me and my house, we will serve the Lord." (Josh. 24:15.)

This is part of the covenant relationship of God with Israel. First with Abram, later with Moses, and then with Joshua, God sought the wholehearted allegiance of Israel. The Lord is a jealous god who will not brook any compromise. If the people will serve him, and him alone, he will continue as their God, but all signs and tokens of other gods must be completely obliterated. Only the Lord God can be served.

We may not like the thought of God's "jealousy," but its meaning is profoundly true. Commitment is total, to God and God alone. "You cannot serve God and mammon." Today we must choose between God the Eternal on one hand and the false gods of our generation on the other. The choice is between God or ambition, God or pride, God or wealth, God or status, God or sex, God or greed, God or family, God or self. The choice is between God or nationalism, God or provincialism, God or racism, God or class, God or culture. The choice is between the God of love and the god of hate, the God of peace and the god of violence, the God of reconciliation and the god of vengeance. It is the judgment of God that none of these false gods can stand alongside him. Our commitment is choosing God and no other. Any other choice is the way of death.

The second of the biblical passages is in the story of the prophet Jeremiah, part of his "great confession." He had been beaten, placed in stocks, thrown into prison, reviled by friend and foe, made the butt of jokes. He spoke the word of God and did not see it come true. Instead the word had become a reproach and derision to Jeremiah, until in his hurt and anger he was ready to quit, but he would not quit.

> If I say, "I will not mention him,
> or speak any more in his name,"

> there is in my heart as it were a burning fire
> shut up in my bones,
> and I am weary with holding it in,
> and I cannot. (Jer. 20:9.)

A divine compulsion moved Jeremiah. He was no longer his own man; he was God's man. But he had not lost his humanity. He was discouraged, angry, depressed. Yet he had committed himself to God. He could not let God down. He would argue with him, he would complain to him, he would vow to ignore him, but the inner fire of God's compelling power was too much for Jeremiah. He was forced to speak the word of God.

Amos knew something of that divine compulsion; he asked:

> The lion has roared;
> who will not fear?
> The Lord God has spoken;
> who can but prophesy? (Amos 3:8.)

Paul too knew the burning fire. He had certain rights which he mentioned in detail, but preaching was not one of them. "For if I preach the gospel, that gives me no ground for boasting. For necessity is laid upon me. Woe to me if I do not preach the gospel!" (I Cor. 9:16.)

Notice that neither of these men became a nonentity. Each kept his own personality, the individuality that God gave him. How often we mistakenly believe that to surrender in commitment to God means to become a blur, a blob, a nothingness, "to be blotted out" as an insignificant worm. It is nothing of the kind. It is to stand erect before men and nations, unashamed, unafraid, unsullied, a man "of God's own choosing," who through the compulsion of that choice gives himself in exclusive and total obedience to God.

Like Jeremiah we will become angry, frustrated, discouraged, and ready to quit. But once having started on the way, once having placed ourselves under God's mandate, we cannot turn back—and live. A woman wrote about the heartache of her marriage:

I do try to love him, not because he is lovable, but because he, too, is a child of God, and I do try to overcome my deep-seated resentment against him for all the things he has done to me, but sometimes I get so tired of trying, when my efforts are so seemingly fruitless. Why must all the efforts and changes come from me? Yet I realize that this trend of thought is just treading on dangerous ground. I know that if I should lose hope and give up trying, I shall not be worth bothering with.

She is worth bothering with, because she is faithful to her commitment to love as God loves. How fine if she knew a warm response to that love! "But he who, having will, yields to the loving urgency of that Life which knocks at his heart, is entered and possessed and transformed and transfigured." [1]

This we see in perfection in Jesus, whose teaching in Mark gives us our third biblical passage: "If any man would come after me, let him deny himself and take up his cross and follow me." (8:34.) Phillips brings out the full meaning of this verse in his translation of the phrase "let him deny himself"; he translates it "he must give up all right to himself." This is complete and total surrender.

It is not enough just to serve God alone, choosing him instead of other gods; nor is it enough just to reveal through one's own real self the burning fire of God's compelling power. One must also give up all right to himself. Like Paul, he must say, "I live; yet not I, but Christ liveth in me." (Gal. 2:20 K.J.V.) Even more, he must say with Jesus, "Not as I will, but as thou wilt."

Here is the full meaning of surrender. I have no "right" to be angry, to be jealous, to be proud. I have only the privilege to love and, in time, to be love.

---

[1] Thomas R. Kelly, *A Testament of Devotion* (New York: Harper & Brothers, 1941), p. 83.

I can claim no rights if I am his. I will not assert myself, telling him what I want him to do for me in return for my surrender. I give myself to him unconditionally, believing that he will give me what I need. I follow him, neither asking the cost nor the goal. I follow him, without telling him I am smart or clever or personable, that I have anything other than myself to give him. He cares nothing about these things. He asks only this, "Do you surrender?"

He comes to us as One unknown, without a name, as of old, by the lakeside, He came to those men who knew Him not. He speaks to us the same word: "Follow thou me!" and sets us to the tasks which He has to fulfil for our time. He commands. And to those who obey Him, whether they be wise or simple, He will reveal Himself in the toils, the conflicts, the sufferings which they shall pass through in His fellowship, and, as an ineffable mystery, they shall learn in their own experience Who He is.[2]

[2] Albert Schweitzer, *The Quest of the Historical Jesus* (London: A. J. C. Black, Ltd., 1922), p. 401.

THE
THIRTIETH WEEK

The Meditation

WHAT A MARVELOUS INSTRUMENT IN THIS BODY OF MINE WHICH THOU HAST given me! Its intricate workings are far beyond my understanding. Through patient research of doctor and scientist I can learn much of its mechanical nature, how it functions through night and day when I am asleep and when I am awake, but thou hast not as yet revealed to the mind of man the full relationship of my body to thought and emotion. I am a spirit clothed with a body, and I am more than my body, but I live and move and have my being through this body thou hast graciously given to me.

Some sincere followers of thy spirit warn me against the dangers of the flesh, suggesting to me that ascetical and puritanical practices to check the body and its desires are thy will. Is it needful for me to condemn my body and its actions, to hold in contempt its desires, to deny my flesh? Is it wrong for me to enjoy good food, to delight in the human form, to celebrate the joys of sensual life, to find recreation in the rhythm of the dance?

Thou hast created this body of mine. Surely it is not to be beaten and condemned in thy name! It is an instrument to be used by thee, to reveal thy love through my love, to show forth thy compassion through my service. It is a thing of glory which can be trained for thy use.

Forgive me when carelessly I disregard my health, physical or mental, thinking these to be no concern of thine. Forgive me, O God, when I use my body solely for me. Forgive me when I refuse to use it in love for others. It is a gift from thee to be spent for thee, that I may grow into a whole person, thy person.

Through my hands, O God, do thy work. Through my feet, walk thy purposes. Through my tongue, speak thou the words of life. May I indeed be a temple of thy spirit, that in my body I may glorify thee.

"Christ has no body on earth now but yours, no hands but yours, no feet but yours. Yours are the eyes through which to look out Christ's compassion to the world. Yours are the feet with which he is to go about doing good, and yours are the hands with which He is to bless us now." (Teresa of Avila)

All or Nothing

(COMMITMENT—3)

Commitment is all or nothing. It is complete surrender, surrender of all we are and all we have. It is total obedience to the law of love as revealed in the God and Father of our Lord Jesus Christ. It is the final act of our life, the offering of self to God.

Yet it is never finished in this life, for it is a constant renewal of our trust and confidence in the God of love. In the beginning of our journey along the Way, when we know so little about God, we can give ourselves only in proportion to that knowledge. As the days and months grow into years, our increasing awareness of the reality of the presence of God is a searchlight seeking out all the hidden corners of our being. As each new hiding place of the self is discovered, we may bring it out into the open of our consciousness, and there dedicate it to God with wholehearted trust.

We also become more sensitive to God's purpose with this growing trust in his love, so that our commitment results in clearer action. What once was quite general, "loving everybody," becomes more specific—a "leading" to call on a certain person, to align oneself with a definite cause, to speak up in a particular matter, to become a con-scientious objector or a militarist, a nationalist or an internationalist, a segregationist or an integrationist.

Now is the time. We have waited long enough, listened long enough, considered long enough. Action is at hand. The choice is to be made, the word spoken, his will done.

"Do you love me?" Jesus asks. Then act. "Come ... deny ... take ... follow." All are words of action. Ask—seek—knock—find—give—serve —love. These are words for all of us. Even those commands to action spoken directly to individuals by Jesus are as much for us today as to them: "Repent, and believe," "Be silent, and come out," "Be clean," "Rise up, take up ... and walk," "Stretch forth," "Go home ... and tell."

Each one of these commands brought forth an act of trust. Boldly, courageously, hopefully, and always confidently, his hearer acted. He surrendered himself, committed himself to the suggested action—and won freedom.

Are you a young person facing the adventure of new life? Jesus in-vites you, "Come, take up your cross, and follow me." For a very few that will mean a Christian profession—minister, missionary. For the rest of us it is to be Christian in whatever vocation is ours. For youth this is a bright new world, where idealism ranks high, where the way of love is a promise of immediate action. So it was that youth followed the Master in days long past. So it is that youth accepts the call to action for today. No special education, no special ability is necessary to follow him. You are to go out with what you have, just as you are. Training and discipline will be added as you commit yourself to him. Will you come to him, follow him, love him?

Are you asking questions about the meaning of life, a young adult, settled in a job, a home, a family, a community? Now what? Where do you go from here? Where is the meaning and purpose in your life?

Are you happy? Are you satisfied with what you are? Are you restless, as though more awaits you?

If happiness is to be poor in spirit, then you must be teachable, not knowing it all, ready to listen and to learn. If happiness is to be pure in heart, then you must be honest and sincere, your yes being yes, your no no. If happiness is to be a peacemaker, then you must put love in action, reconciliation the heart of your life. Are you ready so to act? Will you place yourself in his hands, dedicating your life, your work, your all, to love?

Are you seeking true fellowship, now that the children are gone—a couple together, a widow, a widower, who have come to the peak of your power? Do you have property to offer as a retreat house, money to help educate some boys and girls of promise, time to share with some lonely people, ability to give as a church-school teacher or youth advisor? What are you going to do now with your life, with your money, with your time, with your talents? Are you ready to act, building the kind of fellowship which gains and never loses during your declining years?

The quiet years may be at hand, when peace in its true meaning is becoming yours. You have come, with all your labor, and now you know rest, the refreshment of his spirit. Patient wisdom is yours, not as patient as you may wish, and not as wise as you may hope, yet more than enough for you to be an encouragement to those who still bear the burdens of love. You can praise them, appreciate them, love them. Like Anna, spending her time in the temple, you may be "looking for the redemption of Jerusalem" as you give yourself in blessing to young parents and their children. Are you ready to dedicate yourself anew to the Giver of the peace that passes all understanding?

The word from the Lord is twofold: Rejoice, and again I say, rejoice, and peace, my peace, I give to you. This can be yours.

Seek out a quiet place apart from all others—a chapel, a corner of a sanctuary, your own private place of prayer—and offer this prayer of commitment.

Unto Thee, O God, I present myself. I am what I am. I wish I were more. But I believe thou dost want only what I am, with what I have. Accept this offering of myself, O God of Love, as I come in humble dedication. Blessed be thy name, O God. Amen.

Then rise and go in peace.

THE
THIRTY-FIRST WEEK

The Meditation

I THANK THEE, FATHER, FOR THE GIFT OF LOVE. HOW TERRIBLE TO BE unloved, to sit in the darkness of one's loneliness. Then if ever come the doldrums of the spirit, when days pass with hopeless despair, like a sailing ship caught in a windless sea. Will the gusts of God ever blow again?

Surrounded by a fellowship of love, however, one cannot feel alone. I do not want to be apart from others, a thing set aside, caught in the eddies away from the current of life. I would travel with others in the mainstream of events, taking my rightful place as companion and friend. Forbid, O God, that I should be separate from all others.

Life is more sure for me when I know that even one person loves me. I cannot be all bad, all strange, all queer, when someone loves me. I take courage from love. I believe I can fulfill my responsibilities when someone has faith in me. I feel strong, capable of enduring, for "my strength is as the strength of ten because my heart" is loved.

In the protection of love, O God, I lose my fear of others. With more trust and less suspicion I can accept what seemed to be hostile actions against me. Love is a shield against the darts of fear and anxiety. Especially may I come to thee, O God, and find in thy love home again, the place of love and security, the place of understanding.

Yet I must question this love. Is it only a shell in which to hide? Do I seek such love as a way of escape from the trials of my day?

Would I use love as a means of ending my sense of isolation? Do I need love merely to bring me more assurance that I can face my tasks with honor, protecting my reputation? Is love, even thy love, O Father, for me only a force against estrangement?

Forgive me when I "use" love in any way, O God. Help me to be used by love. Grant that I may turn from a love that seeks for itself to a love that gives of itself. Lead me into the high path of loving rather than into the low path of being loved. Thou art Love, and I would not use thee. I would be used by thee.

Joyous Abandonment

(COMMITMENT—4)

When our commitment is crowned with joy, it reaches its high level of fulfillment. Then the real peace that passes all understanding becomes ours. Then we know with Paul the word of the Lord that cries, "Rejoice . . . and again I will say, Rejoice."

This joy is ours when we pass through surrender to self-abandonment, the free offering of the entire self gladly and willingly made. We go beyond the surrender by which we were forced against our will to capitulate to a superior host. We leave behind us rebellion like that of Jeremiah against the compulsion of the Spirit. We leave behind us the sense of doom against which we cried out for mercy. We turn from pitiful and abject slavery to the joyful acceptance of the submission that alone means full freedom, the freedom of complete trust in and obedience to the providence of God.

A friend in her correspondence wrote of the intense inner struggle to find herself, of the mental and physical anguish that forced her into surrender to God's overwhelming power. Only so could she find the security that she demanded. For three years she fought bitterly, refusing to acquiesce. Then suddenly, she wrote, she abandoned the struggle to assert her own way and in that abandonment found a joy she had never known. "I would be glad to accept the end of all known security," she said, "if that were needed. For now I am free!"

It was such an experience that caused Pascal to write his credo on paper, then pin it to his clothing. For the remainder of his life he wore it much like an amulet. In part this credo declared:

FIRE

God of Abraham, God of Isaac, God of Jacob, not of
    the philosophers and scholars.
Certitude. Certitude. Feeling. Joy. Peace.
God of Jesus Christ.
My God and Thy God.
"Thy God shall be my God."
"Righteous Father, the world hath not known Thee,
    but I have known Thee."
Joy, joy, joy, tears of joy.

More than anyone else the French priest, Pere de Caussade, has expressed this joy in his book *Self-Abandonment to Divine Providence*. In spite of its Roman Catholic theology and its eighteenth-century language it speaks superbly to our condition today. It is both spiritually and psychologically true that only as we live wholly in the present moment can we know the freedom in which security and insecurity are meaningless words. De Caussade calls it, "the Sacrament of the present moment," recognized by us as his moment, and hence, made sacred by him.

What a relief it is to know that this is God's moment, that regardless of how we came to be there, regardless of its circumstances, it is where at the moment he wants us to be. There can only be thanksgiving and rejoicing, then, if it is his moment. Anxiety is a thing of the past, fear is overcome. Perfect love—and perfect trust—cast out all fear. It breeds a courage far from acquiescent pietism, a courage that says with the confidence of the old Indian's prayer, "O Lord, don't let any-thing come that you and I together can't handle!"

Unbelievable power is then released; unexpected legions are seen on the hills surrounding the city. A simplicity of action—fearless, bold, wise, humble—moves the one who knows self-abandonment. He hears his own drummer! His face is set toward Jerusalem. Like Cyrano, "trailing white plumes of freedom," he is "no figure of a man, but a soul clothed in shining armor." He knows true freedom:

> To sing, to laugh, to dream,
> To walk in my own way and be alone,
> Free, with an eye to see things as they are,
> A voice that means manhood—to cock my hat
> Where I choose—At a word, a *Yes,* a *No,*
> To fight—or write. To travel any road
> Under the sun, under the stars, nor doubt
> If fame or fortune lie beyond the bourne—
> Never to make a line I have not heard
> In my own heart; yet, with all modesty
> To say: "My soul, be satisfied with flowers,
> With fruit, with weeds even; but gather them
> In the one garden you may call your own."
>
> .   .   .   .
>
> And if my nature wants the germ that grows
> Towering to heaven like the mountain pine,
> Or like the oak, sheltering multitudes—
> I stand, not high it may be—but alone! [1]

[1] From *Cyrano de Bergerac,* Brian Hooker Translation, by Edmond Rostand. Copyright 1923 by Holt, Rinehart and Winston, Inc. Copyright renewed 1951 by Doris C. Hooker. Reprinted by permission of Holt, Rinehart and Winston, Inc.

THE
THIRTY-SECOND WEEK

The Meditation

"YES GOD! YES GOD! YES, YES AND ALWAYS YES." (NICHOLAS DE CUSA.)

With no qualificataions whatever, with no "yes, but . . ." to dull the edge of my intention, with no "maybe" nor "perhaps" to disclose my doubt, with no "on the other hand" to mark my compromise, I come to thee, my God. Wholly, completely, entirely, utterly I put myself in thy hands. Words cannot contain my commitment to thee.

If this means a new life for me, habits shattered and reformed, my old self removed from the center of my being as thou dost replace me there, the death of the "old man" and the birth of the "new man," blessed be thy name. I ask no salvage of what is left, no mementos of former honors, no souvenirs of past triumphs. What has been is done with, what will be has not come. In the present moment I would live for thee.

If there is struggle and pain for me, O God, in the turning away from old ways with all their security to face new ways in all their uncertainty, blessed be thy name. I do not ask to have the route laid out in full before me, but only that thy light should reveal the next step. Grant to me courage and faith to take that step.

If this means joy and laughter because of trust in thee, a song in the heart, a delight in the coming and the going of the day, a never-ending wonder that thou art God, even my God, blessed be thy name. Thou dost surprise me continually by thyself, by thy visitation in the humble events of my day. Keep me aware of thy presence, O thou holy One.

Here am I. Make my life an affirmation for thee, a light in the darkness, a spring in the desert. "I would fain be to the Eternal Goodness, what his own hand is to a man." (*Theologia Germanica*.)

Growing in the Life of Prayer

At the end of these weeks of intentional practice in the life of prayer, it is good for us to consider how far we have come and how far we may go. Few of us would admit we have grown very much, and none of us would dare say we have arrived. Yet all of us do follow a general pattern of development without our knowledge, levels or stages of growth that have received classical names—purgation, illumination, union. Gerald Heard has called them changes in conduct, in character, and in consciousness, recognizing that progression from stage to stage is varied in each person, but that spiritually and psychologically all who do grow in the life of interior prayer follow this general pattern.

It is certainly neither necessary nor important that all of us examine ourselves to see on what level we now live—preoccupation with growth could become the end of growth—but it is very important to understand why it is in our growing that we have changed and are changing many of our attitudes and practices of prayer. Most of these changes are wholly unconscious, part of the inevitability of growth. Others of them puzzle us, for we find ourselves praying or acting in ways strange to us. Often we may ponder if something is wrong. The truth is, we are maturing spiritually, these being growing pains of our spiritual adolescence. So this presentation will help us to understand ourselves as we continue to grow.

When Paul wrote "pray constantly," he was not suggesting a spate of words. For the apostle prayer was a constant attitude of awareness of the presence of God, to whom he offered himself with rejoicing and thanksgiving. True enough, he had his times of prayer, but they were undergirded and augmented by frequent ejaculations of intercession, of thanksgiving, of adoration, which burst upward from the constancy of that awareness. In similar manner many generations later Brother Lawrence taught that practice of the presence of God, in which continually the offering of himself while preparing a meal, sweeping the floor, or journeying to buy wine for his monastery, as well as during the stated daily hours of worship, was his prayer.

Prayer is far more than a shopping list handed to God with the request, as Gerald Heard has phrased it, "fill this for me in the next five minutes." Nor is it the beggar's cup shaken under the nose of God, as Lillian Smith has so vividly pictured prayer. It can be the constant awareness of God's presence for each one of us who will continue seriously the practice of prayer. Alone, or with others in experimental research through groups, we will discover a series of levels or plateaus of growth in the life of prayer that will lead us to mature prayer, to the prayer that is without ceasing.

BEGINNING PRAYERS

Before the first week has come to a close for some folk, within twenty-four hours for others, an earnest attempt at the practice of prayer will bring a delight, a sense of well-being, a pleasant awareness of inner peace, that is quite surprising to the pray-er. One has a feeling of warmth toward the whole world, as though he wishes to tell everyone what he is finding. After all, results are finally coming through to me through prayer! In other times I have prayed casually, not expecting much—and received no more than that! But now! I want to place my hand on the shoulder of the world, look it in the eye, and say, "Come and see!"

As the weeks of serious practice come one upon the other, most people will find themselves following one of three patterns. Some will seek to remain in that state of delight and well being, hugging their pleasure to themselves. Like Peter of old on the Mount of Transfiguration, they will try to settle down in tents of ecstasy, turning away from the pain of the world. Such an attitude is wrong, for it is essentially a form of pagan contentment. It is truly an opiate of the people, drugging them with sweetness and light.

Others will follow a second pattern. "See what I can do with prayer!" they will exclaim. It becomes a tool in their hands, a tool to move God. They study to learn new techniques by which through the Spirit—they say—they may do wonderful things. This pattern, too, is wrong, for such prayer is but a means to manipulate God, as though man were the master mind and God his servant.

Some folk, however, will find themselves shaken by an inner restlessness. They see as never before the evil in the world. Far more significant, they see the evil that is in themselves. What has been carefully hidden from them is now suddenly revealed. I see how impatient I am, how resentful, how proud, how angry, how unloving. Others have long seen these in me—but not I! Why not? Why have I not known my true self?

This awakening of self-knowledge leads to a searching of one's inner motives. Just why do I do the things I do? Like Paul, we confess that the things we want to do we fail to do and the things we do not want to do, these we do! Who can save us from that death? So we begin to see that we must change ourselves, that we must help others to change themselves.

THE WAY OF SELF-EXAMINATION

Then it is that we begin to move onto a new plateau of prayer. We do pray for others, but our prayers are mostly for ourselves. Yet how ineffective they seem to be; there are no results as far as I am concerned. How sinful I am! No longer does the phrase "miserable sinner" offend me. The eternal God is beginning to reveal my sins to me. Becoming more sensitive to his love, I know how far I have traveled from his house.

At the same time we discover that we are growing less critical of others. Our harsh judgments, our unfair comparisons, our unloving criticism that we have used to build up ourselves as we tear down others suddenly are gone. Some of us for years deliberately have tried to control or even to eliminate these critical thoughts or words, but we have found the task almost too much for us. Now, without conscious effort on our part, often without any thought of it at all, we are amazed to notice that days or even weeks have gone by—and not once has there been as much as a tiny criticism. Our learning to pray for others, with the love that must go along with such intercession, plus the certain awareness of our own sinful thoughts and actions, have changed our entire ways of thinking and of speaking. What we had tried through human willing to bring under control suddenly is no more. Through God's grace alone has come the beginning of the end of all critical thought and action. Blessed be his name!

In this purging of self as we learn to love others and God, we find also that we are becoming keenly sensitive to God's will. We begin to "listen" to the voice within and then to follow it. Each day's triumph in following that voice, no matter how simple its call may be, makes that much easier the next day's victory. For most of us no difficult choices face us day by day. We heed his leading in the simple routine by which through his grace we find our life. That day by day practice of listening to and heeding his will—at first the result of conscious action, but later the inevitable fruit of our growing understanding of God as we begin to understand ourselves—is the preparation for the difficult choices that sooner or later will upset our day. Then we will know to wait, not to make a move of any kind unless action is immediately demanded, and then to move only after our best thinking. We will make mistakes; time and again our choice may prove to be the wrong one in the light of subsequent events, but each experiment in following his will teaches us to listen carefully, to weight cautiously, to act boldly.

This increasing sensitivity to his will gives us a new sense of moral values. Outer conformity to the mores of our culture is far less important to us. After all, knowing ourselves as we now begin to we wonder that we are not continually being caught by our own evil. That new thought in turn helps us refuse to condemn others, as we have already seen. I know, one says, that if I were in his shoes, I would have been a greater sinner.

Inner motives and inner attitudes become the important ones. We see that our pride, our resentful manner, our unlovingness, our thoughtlessness, and the like are the true sins of the spirit. Not the law of man but the law of God—this we must not disobey. Not because of fear, not because we are afraid God will punish us, but because of our love for him. The perfect love that casts out all fear is slowly but surely coming alive in us.

Strangely enough, this new understanding of ourselves and of the love of God often creates a puzzlement that disturbs many of us. We find it now a real task to pray. Frequently we are touched with the mood of spiritual dryness in which the act of getting acquainted with ourselves proves to be most tedious. The joy and delight of our beginning prayers turns into plodding routine as we see with new revelations our many-sidedness. It is as Dr. Harry Emerson Fosdick wrote years ago: "I should know myself better if there were not so many of me."

Some of us, refusing for a time to admit that we are legion, may find escape as one young woman did. In her prayer group she reported that she had covered a mirror in her kitchen with a towel. "I just could not look at myself any more," she continued. "What I was beginning to see made me ashamed." Then she went on to say with a laugh, "But I couldn't hide myself from me!"

This movement of prayer on the plateau of self-examination is much like our experience with marriage. The first delights of the honeymoon pass, and the necessary adjustments between two people begin. There are always some who wonder if it is worthwhile continuing a marriage when the delights of the early months and years have ended. Such folk may seek relief in divorce. But those who hold on through the testing years, knowing that true love is yet underneath the dryness of routine days and nights, will some day know what real marriage can be.

So it is that some of us, no longer finding the pleasure and delight of early weeks and months of serious practice of prayer, are ready to drift along. We have learned much of value that we just cannot let go. We hope to remain at that level. A few actually do stop their search, turning their backs upon prayer. For both groups this means the ending of growth.

THE WAY OF ILLUMINATION

Those who do persist in the life of prayer will gradually become aware of a climb to another plateau. Their own weakness and sin are still evident. There is no lessening of that sad recognition. Yet, like Isaiah of old, having seen the King, the Lord of hosts, and having accepted the forgiveness of the coal that purged the evil of their lips, they know as never before the deep love of God within the inner heart.

They have turned away from much praying for the self. The prayer of petition, the "give me" that was so prevalent earlier—even the later requests for courage, wisdom, patience, and insight—almost completely disappear. Instead, there is the prayer of commitment: "Accept me, use me, serve through me." Along with this new kind of petition, this offering of self, is a more attentive listening to God's will, a clearer certainty of his leading through all the events of one's day. Because we are learning to listen more and more, our prayers are far less specific than before. Words become of little importance, and the few we use no longer try to "tell" God what we wish to do or to suggest to him what we think he ought to do. For many of us words, vocal or mental, are but in the way as we learn to rest in the light of his spirit.

"To rest"? Not quite. The Mary-of-the-inner-spirit, though still being fed at the feet of the Master, rises to serve gladly with the Martha-of-the-inner-spirit. Visiting the sick or the lonely; sharing in church or denomination as teacher, choir member, officer, committee drudge; volunteering in the life of the community as Red Cross worker, Gray Lady, scout leader, car driver, ward helper, and a host of other things— these are but a few of the ways we show our love for God. In this service a new delight flows through us, less rosy than that at the beginning of our life of prayer, but more radiant. Our happiness has grown into joy. We know deep within that through his grace we are being used by God.

Concomitant with the enlarging sphere of service is a remarkable sense of sympathy toward and understanding of others. Our warm outreach to others can best be revealed in our deepening feeling of inadequacy before the love of God. True enough, others around us may be quite terrible in their human relationships, but really, we are worse. Knowing ourselves as we do, we just cannot condemn the actions of others as once we did. It is not so much the negative attitude of being less critical of others which we found within ourselves in the second plateau of prayer as it is the positive attitude of kinship with others, love for others. There is a tendering of spirit that frequently brings wet eyes. Ashamedly at times we may try to hide the tears, but they are God's gift of love, washing clean our selfish vision. Because of those folk around us, friends and strangers, we lift a hundred little aspirations daily—prayers of intercession, of thanksgiving, of adoration, of blessing.

In the continuing sense of God's presence we now come to know the full meaning of creative silence. Still we will read many books, but in the quiet of our solitude we will not hasten like before to grab a book lest we be alone for a moment. We will begin to read a spiritual classic, and then will find that for thirty minutes, even an hour, we have sat in deep silence, "looking at God, and God looking at me," as the peasant told the Cure d'Ars. The heart has truly entered into our reading.

This is indeed a high level of prayer. The fulfillment of our love for God is attained by our love for our fellow man. The light of his spirit truly shines on our pathway.

THE WAY OF CONTEMPLATION

Then it is, through the grace of God, that we emerge upon a new plateau of prayer. Neither depression nor ecstasy touches us. The former zigzag of ups and downs is replaced by an undulation of mood that rests upon a norm of assurance in the providence and care of God. We no longer are important; only he has meaning and reality. Yet we know less than ever about the wonder of God. As Douglas Steere has said in *On Listening to Another*: "In the adoration of him, we find ourselves always quivering before a mysterious depth that we cannot get to the bottom of." [1]

Now we begin to realize that our whole life is a prayer. Words spoken or thought are very rare, but our commitment becomes as complete as we can make it, being renewed, refreshened every day. Paul's words, "Pray constantly," have become real.

There is almost no praying for the self, not for things, not for qualities of character, not even that God will use us. The whole life is an offering made gladly to God, in which the full prayer of Jesus, "Not as I will, but as thou wilt," alone fills our inner being. Yet these words are seldom thought. They have become part of our very selves and need no expression.

So, too, there is almost no praying for others. It is not that we no longer wish to intercede. Rather, it is that we no longer need to do so. Our life is an intercession, our prayer is our love, and our love is our prayer. All the folk we know are offered to God, held in the Light, surrounded by the Light, one with the Light. Friend and foe have

[1] New York: Harper & Brothers, 1955, p. 42.

become one with us, one with God. We can say no words. They have become a hindrance. Like Seraphim of Sarov, "we must pray only until God the Holy Spirit descends. . . . when he comes to visit us, we must cease to pray." [2]

For a rare handful of folk the prayers of quiet, of union, are yet to come; these are plateaus beyond most of us. But these four levels are ours, the gifts of God as we grow. The life of prayer is one of continual dynamic growth, ever-changing, ever-moving toward oneness with God. It is essentially commitment, a life lived in and for God.

[2] *Ibid.*, p. 45.

BIBLIOGRAPHY

These books are the "foundation" volumes for the devotional section of a church or a personal library. They are arranged by groupings so as to make more valuable their use for quick reference. All of those listed under "Group Use" are in print as of April, 1962. Though some of the other books are out of print—and are marked "O. P."—they are worth borrowing from a library or purchasing as used copies if possible.

I. GROUP USE
  A. For Prayer Classes
    1. Beginning Classes
      Day, Albert Edward. *Discipline and Discovery*. Rev. ed. Nashville: Disciplined Order of Christ, 1961.
      Freer, Harold Wiley and Hall, Francis B. *Two or Three Together*. New York: Harper & Brothers, 1954.
      Keene, J. Calvin. *Meditations on the Gospels*. Nashville: Abingdon Press, 1959.
      Sangster, W. E. *The Secret of Radiant Life*. Nashville: Abingdon Press, 1957.
      Trueblood, Elton. *Confronting Christ*. New York: Harper & Brothers, 1960.
    2. Continuing Classes
      Fénelon, François. *Christian Perfection*. Edited by Charles F. Whiston. New York: Harper & Brothers, 1947.
      Freer, Harold Wiley. *Christian Disciplines*. New York: Pageant Press, 1960.
      Heard, Gerald. *Prayers and Meditations*. New York: Harper & Brothers, 1949.
      Kepler, Thomas S., editor. *Theologia Germanica*. Cleveland, Ohio: The World Publishing Company.
      Law, William. *A Serious Call to a Devout and Holy Life*. Edited by John Meister. Philadelphia: The Westminster Press.
      Matson, Archie. *A Month with the Master*. New York: Harper & Brothers, 1958.
      Thomas a Kempis. *The Imitation of Christ*. Various editions.
  B. For Discussion Groups
    1. The Life of Prayer

Coburn, John B. *Prayer and Personal Religion.* Philadelphia: The Westminster Press, 1957.

Heard, Gerald. *The Preface to Prayer.* New York: Harper & Brothers, 1944.

Heiler, Friedrich. *Prayer.* New York: Oxford University Press, 1958.

Kelly, Thomas. *A Testament of Devotion.* New York: Harper & Brothers, 1941.

Parker, William R., and Dare, Elaine St. Johns. *Prayer Can Change Your Life.* Englewood Cliffs, N. J.: Prentice-Hall, Inc., 1957.

Radcliffe, Lynn J. *Making Prayer Real.* Nashville: Abingdon Press, 1952.

Stewart, George Shaw. *The Lower Levels of Prayer.* Nashville: Abingdon Press, 1939; paper back.

Wyon, Olive. *The School of Prayer.* London: Student Christian Movement Press, 1947.

2. Prayer and the Self

Bonhoeffer, Dietrich. *The Cost of Discipleship.* New York: The Macmillan Company.

Fromm, Erich. *Psychoanalysis and Religion.* New Haven, Conn.: Yale University Press, 1959.

Loomis, Earl A., Jr. *The Self in Pilgrimage.* New York: Harper & Brothers, 1960.

Martin, P. W. *Experiment in Depth.* London: Routledge and Kegan Paul, Ltd., 1955.

Progoff, Ira. *Depth Psychology and Modern Man.* New York: Julian Press.

Roberts, David E. *Psychotherapy and a Christian View of Man.* New York: Charles Scribner's Sons, 1950.

Tournier, Paul. *The Meaning of Persons.* New York: Harper & Brothers, 1957.

II. INDIVIDUAL READING

A. Daily Devotions

Baillie, John. *A Diary of Private Prayer.* New York: Charles Scribner's Sons.

————. *Diary of Readings.* New York: Charles Scribner's Sons, 1955.

Bowie, Walter Russell. *Christ Be with Me.* Nashville: Abingdon Press, 1958.

Chambers, Oswald. *My Utmost for His Highest.* New York: Dodd, Mead & Company, 1935.

Fosdick, Harry Emerson. *Three Meanings*. New York: Association Press, 1950.

Harkness, Georgia. *Through Christ Our Lord*. Nashville: Abingdon Press, 1950.

Listen, the Lord. Santa Fe, N. M.: Rydal Press.

Lyon, Quinter M., editor. *Quiet Strength from World Religions*. New York: Harper & Brothers, 1960.

Oldham, J. H. *A Devotional Diary*. New York: Harper & Brothers.

Rhoades, Winfred, editor. *To Know God Better*. New York: Harper & Brothers, 1958.

Russell, A. J., editor. *God Calling: A Devotional Diary*. New York: Dodd, Mead & Company.

B. Spiritual Biographies

Camus, Jean Pierre. *The Spirit of St. François de Sales*. Translated by C. F. Kelley. New York: Harper & Brothers, 1952.

Cheney, Sheldon. *Men Who Have Walked with God*. New York: Alfred A. Knopf, Inc., 1945.

Cropper, Margaret. *The Life of Evelyn Underhill*. New York: Harper & Brothers, 1958.

Day, Dorothy. *The Long Loneliness*. New York: Harper & Brothers, 1952.

Irvine, Alexander. *My Lady of the Chimney Corner*. New York: William Collins Sons & Company.

Jackson, Frances E. *The Loneliest Journey*. Philadelphia: The Westminster Press. O. P.

Lester, Muriel. *It Occurred to Me*. New York: Harper & Brothers, 1937. O. P.

——————. *It So Happened*. New York: Harper & Brothers, 1947. O. P.

Oldham, J. H. *Florence Allshorn*. New York: Harper & Brothers, 1952.

Powell, Cyril H. *Secrets of Answered Prayer*. New York: Thomas Y. Crowell Company, 1960.

Smith, Lillian. *The Journey*. Cleveland, Ohio: The World Publishing Company.

Woolman, John. *The Journal of John Woolman*. Edited by Thomas S. Kepler. Cleveland, Ohio: The World Publishing Company.

C. Spiritual Direction

Caussade, Jean Pierre de. *Abandonment to Divine Providence*. New York: Templegate Publishers.

——————. *Spiritual Letters*. New York: Templegate Publishers.

Chapman, John. *Spiritual Letters of John Chapman.* New York: Sheed & Ward, Inc., 1959; paper edition.

Fénelon, François. *Letters to Men and Women.* Westminster, Md.: Newman Press, 1957.

Hugel, Friedrich von. Edited by Gwendolen Greene. *Letters to a Niece.* Chicago: Henry Regnery Company, 1955.

Leen, Edward. *Progress Through Mental Prayer.* New York: Sheed & Ward, Inc.

Tourville, Abbe de. *Letters of Direction.* New York: Thomas Y. Crowell Company, 1939.

Underhill, Evelyn. *Letters of Evelyn Underhill,* ed. Charles Williams. New York: Longmans, Green & Company, 1943.

D. Prayer and Healing

Boggs, Wade H., Jr. *Faith Healing and the Christian Faith.* Richmond, Va.: John Knox Press, 1956.

Large, John E. *The Ministry of Healing.* New York: Morehouse-Barlow Company, 1959.

Martin, Bernard. *The Healing Ministry in the Church.* Richmond, Va.: John Knox Press, 1960.

Sanford, Agnes. *The Healing Light.* St. Paul, Minn.: Macalester Park Publishing Company, 1947.

Sanford, Edgar L. *God's Healing Power.* Englewood Cliffs, N. J.: Prentice-Hall, Inc., 1959.

Weatherhead, Leslie D. *Psychology, Religion and Healing.* Rev. ed. Nashville: Abingdon Press, 1954.

E. Spiritual Classics

Angelus Silesius. *The Cherubinic Wanderer.* New York: Pantheon Books, 1953.

Augustine. *Confessions of St. Augustine.* Various editions.

Backhouse, William, and Janson, James, editors. *A Guide to True Peace.* New York: Harper & Brothers, 1956.

Baker, Augustine. *Holy Wisdom.* New York: Harper & Brothers, 1949. O. P.

Bernardino de Laredo. *The Ascent of Mount Sion.* Translated by E. Allison Peers. New York: Harper & Brothers, 1952. O. P.

Boehme, Jakob. *The Way to Christ.* Translated by John Joseph Stoudt. New York: Harper & Brothers, 1947. O. P.

Chambers, P. Franklin. *Juliana of Norwich.* New York: Harper & Brothers, 1956.

Eckhart, Meister. *Meister Eckhart.* Edited and translated by Raymond B. Blakney. New York: Harper & Brothers, 1941.

Fénelon, François. *Christian Perfection*. Edited by Charles F. Whiston. New York: Harper & Brothers, 1947.

Francis de Sales. *Introduction to a Devout Life*. Edited by Thomas S. Kepler. Cleveland, Ohio: The World Publishing Company.

——————. *The Spirit of Love*. New York: Harper & Brothers. O. P.

——————. *Spiritual Maxims*. Edited by C. F. Kelley. New York: Harper & Brothers, 1953.

Grou, Jean-Nicolas. *How to Pray*. New York: Harper & Brothers, 1956.

Herman, E. *Creative Prayer*. New York: Harper & Brothers, 1934.

Hilton, Walter. *The Goad of Love*. New York: Harper & Brothers O. P.

John Climacus, St. *The Ladder of Divine Ascent*. New York: Harper & Brothers, 1959.

Kadloubovsky, E., and Palmer, G. E. H., editors. *Writings from the Philokalia on Prayer of the Heart*. London: Faber & Faber, Ltd., 1951.

Kelpius, Johannes. *A Method of Prayer*. Edited by E. Gordon Alderfer. New York: Harper & Brothers.

Kierkegaard, Søren. *Purity of Heart*. Translated by Douglas V. Steere. New York: Harper & Brothers, 1956; paper edition.

Law, William. *A Serious Call to a Devout and Holy Life*. Edited by John Meister. Philadelphia: The Westminster Press.

Pietro Damiani, St. *Selected Writings on the Spiritual Life*. New York: Harper & Brothers, 1960.

Progoff, Ira, editor. *The Cloud of Unknowing*. New York: Julian Press.

Richard of St. Victor. *Selected Writings on Contemplation*. New York: Harper & Brothers, 1957.

Ruysbroeck, Jan van. *The Spiritual Espousals*. Translated by Eric Colledge. New York: Harper & Brothers, 1953. O. P.

Scupoli, Lawrence. *The Spiritual Combat*. Westminster, Md.: Newman Press, 1945.

Suso, Heinrich. *Little Book of Eternal Wisdom* and *Little Book of Truth*. Translated by James M. Clark. New York: Harper & Brothers, 1953. O. P.

Thomas a Kempis. *The Imitation of Christ*. Various editions.

Traherne, Thomas. *Centuries*. New York: Harper & Brothers, 1960.

The Way of a Pilgrim and *The Pilgrim Continues His Way*. Greenwich, Conn.: The Seabury Press.

William of St. Thierry. *Meditations*. New York: Harper & Brothers, 1954.

F. Children's Devotions
  1. Younger Children
    Jones, Jessie Orton, editor. *Small Rain*. New York: The Viking Press, 1943.
    Orleans, Ilo. *This Wonderful Day*. New York: Union of American Hebrew Congregations, 1958.
    Paradis, Adrian and Grace. *Grow in Grace*. Nashville: Abingdon Press, 1958.
    Tudor, Tasha. *First Graces*. New York: Henry Z. Walck, Inc.
    —————. *First Prayers*. New York: Henry Z. Walck, Inc.
  2. Older Children
    Welker, Edith Frances and Barber, Aimee Angus. *Thoughts of God for Boys and Girls*. New York: Harper & Brothers, 1948.
    Wilson, Jim. *First Steps in Meditation for Young People*. London: James Clarke & Company.

G. General Devotional Reading
  Bauman, Edward. *Intercessory Prayer*. Philadelphia: The Westminster Press, 1958.
  Belden, Albert D. *The Practice of Prayer*. New York: Harper & Brothers, 1954.
  Bonnell, John S. *The Practice and Power of Prayer*. Philadelphia: The Westminster Press, 1954.
  Boone, J. Allen. *Kinship with All Life*. New York: Harper & Brothers, 1954.
  Bro, Marguerite Harmon. *More Than We Are*. New York: Harper & Brothers, 1948.
  Buber, Martin. *To Hallow This Life*. Edited by Jacob Trapp. New York: Harper & Brothers, 1958.
  Burkhart, Roy. *The Secret of Life*. New York: Harper & Brothers.
  Buttrick, George. *Prayer*. Nashville: Abingdon Press, 1957; Apex edition.
  Casteel, John L. *Rediscovering Prayer*. New York: Association Press.
  —————. *Spiritual Renewal through Personal Groups*. New York: Association Press, 1957.
  Colliander, Tito. *The Way of the Ascetics*. Translated by Katharine Ferré. New York: Harper & Brothers, 1961.
  Day, Albert Edward. *An Autobiography of Prayer*. New York: Harper & Brothers, 1952.
  —————. *Dialogue and Destiny*. New York: Harper & Brothers, 1961.
  —————. *Existence under God*. Nashville: Abingdon Press. 1958.

Ferré, Nels F. S. *Making Religion Real*. New York: Harper & Brothers, 1955.

——————. *Strengthening the Spiritual Life*. New York: Harper & Brothers, 1951.

Fromm, Erich. *The Art of Loving*. New York: Harper & Brothers, 1956.

Goldsmith, Joel S. *The Art of Meditation*. New York: Harper & Brothers, 1957.

Harkness, Georgia. *Prayer and the Common Life*. Nashville: Abingdon Press, 1948.

Heard, Gerald. *Training in the Life of the Spirit*. New York: Harper & Brothers.

Huxley, Aldous. *The Perennial Philosophy*. New York: Harper & Brothers, 1945.

James, Joseph, editor. *The Way of Mysticism*. New York: Harper & Brothers, 1951. O. P.

Kelly, Thomas. *A Testament of Devotion*. New York: Harper & Brothers, 1941.

McLachlan, Lewis. *Intelligent Prayer*. London: James Clarke & Company, 1946.

——————. *The Teachings of Jesus on Prayer*. London: James Clarke & Company, 1952.

Magee, John. *Reality and Prayer*. New York: Harper & Brothers, 1957.

Phillips, Dorothy B., *et al.*, editors. *The Choice Is Always Ours*. Rev. ed. New York: Harper & Brothers, 1960.

Raynolds, Robert. *The Choice to Love*. New York: Harper & Brothers, 1959.

——————. *In Praise of Gratitude*. New York: Harper & Brothers, 1961.

Steere, Douglas V. *On Beginning from Within*. New York: Harper & Brothers, 1943.

——————. *On Listening to Another*. New York: Harper & Brothers, 1955.

——————. *Work and Contemplation*. New York: Harper & Brothers, 1957.

Stewart, George Shaw. *The Lower Levels of Prayer*. Nashville: Abingdon Press, 1939; paper back.

Strong, Mary, editor. *Letters of the Scattered Brotherhood*. New York: Harper & Brothers.

Thurman, Howard. *Deep Is the Hunger*. New York: Harper & Brothers, 1951.

——————. *The Growing Edge.* New York: Harper & Brothers, 1956.

——————. *The Inward Journey.* New York: Harper & Brothers, 1961.

——————. *Meditations of the Heart.* New York: Harper & Brothers, 1953.

Trueblood, Elton. *Alternative to Futility.* New York: Harper & Brothers, 1948.

——————. *The Company of the Committed.* New York: Harper & Brothers, 1961.

Underhill, Evelyn. *Fruits of the Spirit, Light of Christ, and Abba.* New York: Longmans, Green & Company, 1956.

——————. *Concerning the Inner Life, and House of the Soul.* New York: E. P. Dutton & Company.

——————. *The Golden Sequence.* New York: Harper & Brothers, 1960.

——————. *The Mount of Purification.* New York: Longmans, Green & Company, 1960.

——————. *Mysticism.* New York: E. P. Dutton & Company, 1930.

——————. *Practical Mysticism.* New York: E. P. Dutton & Company.

——————. *School of Charity, and Mystery of Sacrifice.* New York: Longmans, Green & Company, 1954.

——————. *The Spiritual Life.* New York: Harper & Brothers, 1955.

Weatherhead, Leslie D. *A Private House of Prayer.* Nashville: Abingdon Press, 1959.

——————. *The Will of God.* Nashville: Abingdon Press, 1944.

Whiston, Charles. *Teach Us to Pray.* Boston: Pilgrim Press, 1949.

Wyon, Olive. *The School of Prayer.* London: Student Christian Movement Press, 1947.

That we may attain the highest plateau of prayer, here is a series of prayer lessons to help us progress from elementary self-centered prayers to God-centered prayers. When this point is reached, "there is almost no praying for the self, not for things, not for qualities of character, not even that God will use us. The whole life is an offering made gladly to God, in which the full prayer of Jesus, 'Not as I will, but as thou wilt,' alone fills our inner being."

The 32 weekly lessons move forward through six major kinds of prayer: thanksgiving, confession, forgiveness, intercession, adoration, and commitment. Divided into two parts, each lesson contains a prayer-meditation, spoken directly to God, and an exercise with illustrative stories and quotations. Specific suggestions for practice during the week ahead are at the close of each chapter.

Through the use of these resources, individuals and groups seeking to lift their prayer life to the highest level will learn how to pray inwardly, to intercede for others, to experience personal encounter with God, and to practice his presence at all times.